ZENITH

Dr Ajay Data is an entrepreneur, technologist and global internet leader, known for his pioneering work in multilingual internet, artificial intelligence and enterprise communication technologies. He serves as the Managing Director of the Data Group of Industries, which operates diverse ventures in technology, edible oils and enterprise solutions.

Ajay holds the distinction of being India's first elected member of the ccNSO Council of ICANN (Internet Corporation for Assigned Names and Numbers), where he contributed significantly to global internet policymaking. He also co-chaired the Neo-Brahmi Generation Panel, which created the official language rules for domain names in Indian scripts—rules that are now embedded in the Root Zone of the Domain Name System (DNS), enabling a truly multilingual internet.

He is globally recognized for launching the world's first linguistic email platform supporting addresses in Indian languages, bringing digital inclusion to millions. His leadership in Universal Acceptance and commitment to an inclusive internet have earned him awards such as the Aegis Graham Bell Award for Innovation.

Through his ventures, public service and mentorship, Ajay continues to advocate for ethical AI, inclusive technology and scalable innovation. In this book, he empowers readers to harness the power of artificial intelligence through practical and role-based prompt engineering—making the future of work more accessible to all.

Connect with him on
Twitter: https://x.com/ajaydata/
Instagram: https://www.instagram.com/ajaydata/
LinkedIn: https://www.linkedin.com/in/ajaykdata

ZENITH

MASTERING AI FOR
EVERYDAY LIFE AND WORK

AJAY DATA

RUPA

Published by
Rupa Publications India Pvt. Ltd 2025
7/16, Ansari Road, Daryaganj
New Delhi 110002

Sales centres:
Bengaluru Chennai Hyderabad
Jaipur Kathmandu Kolkata
Mumbai Prayagraj

P-ISBN: 978-93-7003-751-9
E-ISBN: 978-93-7003-279-8

First impression 2025

10 9 8 7 6 5 4 3 2 1

The moral right of the author has been asserted.

Printed in India

Contents

Foreword

In a world increasingly driven by technology, staying relevant demands not just adaptability but also the ability to leverage innovation effectively. *Zenith: Mastering AI for Everyday Life and Work* is a pivotal resource in this landscape, equipping readers with the tools to unlock the full potential of artificial intelligence (AI).

Throughout my career—as Chief Financial Officer (CFO) and board member at Infosys, Chairman of Manipal Global Education, and Co-Founder of the Akshaya Patra Foundation and now as a venture capitalist—I have witnessed first-hand how technology transforms industries and empowers individuals. As the AI era unfolds, the ability to craft precise and impactful prompts has become a cornerstone skill for fostering productivity, creativity and success.

Ajay Data, an innovator entrepreneur with a distinguished background in technology and business, brings unparalleled insight into this emerging field. His expertise in blending innovation with practicality ensures that this book offers something for everyone—from professionals and educators to entrepreneurs and individuals seeking personal growth. By providing a road map for harnessing AI through simple and advanced prompts, Data has made a complex subject approachable and impactful for all.

In an era where the convergence of technology, culture and human values shapes every facet of our lives, this book is a timely guide. It not only demystifies the art of prompt engineering but also empowers readers to seamlessly integrate AI into their workflows, unlocking efficiency and creativity like never before.

I am happy to introduce a work that aligns with the principles I have endeavoured to uphold throughout my career: fostering knowledge, innovation and growth for a brighter future.

—T.V. Mohandas Pai
Chairman, Aarin Capital Partners

Foreword

In an era where technology is deeply interwoven into the fabric of our daily lives, the ability to effectively communicate with AI has become a pivotal skill. Over my decades of work at the Information Society Research programme managed by the European Commission, and in the field of internet governance in the decades after, I have seen the critical role of effective communication in harnessing the potential of technology.

Ajay Data's book serves as a comprehensive manual for navigating the complexities of AI interaction. It provides readers with practical tools and strategies to engage with AI systems across various domains.

A particularly compelling aspect of this work is its emphasis on inclusivity. By demystifying the art of prompt engineering, Data empowers readers from diverse backgrounds to unlock new levels of productivity, creativity and efficiency. This approach not only democratizes access to AI technologies but also fosters a more inclusive digital environment, emphasizing the value of application in different domains.

I am confident that readers will find *Zenith: Mastering AI for Everyday Life and Work* to be a valuable resource and inspiration in their journey towards mastering the language of AI and harnessing its potential to create a more inclusive and connected world.

—Maarten Botterman
Chair, Global Forum for Cyber Expertise Working Group
on Emerging Technologies;
Member of the ICANN Board;
Independent Strategic Advisor on Internet Governance

Preface

As Managing Director of the Data Group, my life is often a whirlwind of activity, managing diverse businesses ranging from mustard oil, refined oil and vegetable oil to the dynamic world of information technology—all under an umbrella of companies employing over 5,000 people.

My daily schedule isn't just consumed by my own businesses; a significant portion of my time is also devoted to contributing to various organizations such as TiE, the Entrepreneurs' Organization, ICANN, and other local and global initiatives. I am deeply involved in fostering the start-up ecosystem and supporting innovation wherever I can.

One Monday, I received a call from RJ Mohit, a well-known radio personality who had recently ventured into podcasting. He invited me to be his first guest, and I happily agreed to support his new journey. That podcast turned out to be a fascinating conversation, with snippets shared on social media, including one reel on Instagram that unexpectedly went viral. The reel, which focused on prompt engineering, garnered nearly 6 million views.

In the reel, I shared how prompt engineering has the power to not only enhance abilities but also secure jobs, create rewarding opportunities and elevate social status of individuals. Its message resonated widely, and the popularity of the reel led to an influx of messages from people asking what prompt engineering is and how it works.

Initially, I tried to guide them by searching for resources online. To my surprise, I found very little that was easy to understand and accessible to the average person. This gap inspired me to take action. I realized the need to create a resource that could demystify prompt engineering and equip people with the tools to thrive in this new era of artificial intelligence (AI).

This book is the result of that realization. Writing it presented its own challenges. Prompt engineering is a relatively new concept, and I needed to ensure the content was both comprehensive and accessible. I conducted extensive research and studied the field deeply, but I also sought validation and insights from experts in AI.

This book is not just a guide; it is a journey into the transformative power of AI. I hope this book empowers you as much as it has inspired me.

Introduction

As we enter an era defined by technological transformation, AI is poised to reshape the way we live, work and think. The impact of AI is no longer confined to futuristic aspirations—it's here, woven into the fabric of our daily lives, influencing everything from mundane tasks to groundbreaking innovations. But, like any powerful tool, the true potential of AI lies in how we wield it. Unlocking this potential starts with understanding the art of communicating with AI effectively.

This book is your gateway to unleashing the transformative power of AI through the practice of prompt engineering. At its core, prompt engineering is the ability to craft precise, meaningful inputs that guide AI systems towards desired outputs. Think of it as learning the dialect of a revolutionary new tool—one that translates your ideas and goals into actionable, intelligent responses. Whether you're an entrepreneur igniting innovation, a teacher reimagining education, or simply a curious individual, mastering this skill can redefine how you interact with technology.

Technology's true potential is realized not by passive use but by intentional engagement—using it to amplify human creativity, problem-solving and productivity. Just as the internet, mobile and cloud computing catalysed new paradigms of progress, AI represents the next frontier in application design, governance and optimization. This book transcends the technical, offering a philosophical and practical approach to integrating AI into your life and work. It's a call to action—a chance to collaborate with AI as a partner in your journey of growth.

Through these pages you'll discover the methods, strategies and insights needed to make AI work for you, seamlessly and purposefully. By learning to craft precise prompts, you'll unlock the ability to solve complex problems, spark your imagination and achieve more in less time. The skills shared here will equip you not just for today's technological landscape but for the dynamic, AI-driven future ahead.

Dive in, explore the possibilities and embrace AI as an enabler of human potential. Together, let's turn AI into a tool that enhances—not replaces—our creativity and ambition.

1

Introduction to Prompt Engineering

IMAGINE BEING ABLE TO TALK to your computer or smartphone and have it understand exactly what you need, every time. Whether it's finding the perfect recipe, drafting an email or creating a travel plan, AI is now making this possible. However, to get the best results from AI, we need to know how to communicate with it effectively. This skill is called 'prompt engineering'. Just as we learn how to ask the right questions in real life, prompt engineering teaches us how to ask AI the right questions to get useful answers.

In this chapter, we'll dive into what prompt engineering is, why it's important, and how you can start using it in your everyday life. Whether you're a student, professional or simply someone who enjoys exploring technology, learning how to create clear and effective prompts can make your interactions with AI more helpful and enjoyable.[1]

What is prompt engineering?

Prompt engineering is simply the practice of crafting commands or questions for an AI system in a way that helps it understand and respond accurately. Think of it like giving directions: the clearer your instructions, the easier it is for the other person to follow. In this case, AI is the 'other person' who will act based on what we ask it to do.

---

[1]For an overview of various AI tools/large language models (LLMs), refer to the last chapter.

When we talk to an AI, such as ChatGPT or Gemini or Copilot, on our phones or computers, we're using prompts to guide it. Good prompts can make the difference between getting a vague, unhelpful response and a detailed, relevant one. With a little practice, anyone can learn how to create prompts that give better results.

Why prompt engineering matters

With prompt engineering, you don't need to be a tech expert to use AI effectively. Whether it's drafting documents, generating ideas or solving problems, prompt engineering allows you to make the most of AI's capabilities with simple instructions.

Incorrect prompt: Newton's law?

Correct prompt: Explain Newton's First Law of Motion in simple terms, with an example for better understanding.

Here are a few reasons why mastering this skill is important:

- **Saves time**: Well-crafted prompts give more accurate responses, reducing the need to query multiple times.
- **Increases productivity**: You can use AI to handle routine tasks or brainstorm ideas quickly.
- **Personalizes results**: A well-designed prompt lets AI understand your preferences and tailor responses accordingly.

Now, let's explore the key elements of creating effective prompts.

How to craft effective prompts

Be clear and direct

When talking to AI, clarity is essential. AI doesn't 'guess' the way a human might. It relies on the words you give it. To get the most accurate answer, keep your prompts clear and specific.

Example

Instead of asking, 'Tell me about climate change', you could say, 'Explain climate change and its effects on coastal cities in simple terms'.

The more specific you are, the better AI will understand what you need.

Provide context

Context helps AI understand the situation better, leading to more relevant answers. This can include setting the scene or mentioning who the response is for. Context can make a big difference, especially if you're working on something complex.

Example

If you say, 'Write a workout plan', the response might be too general. But by adding context—'Write a workout plan for a beginner who wants to lose weight and has only 20 minutes each day'—you help AI focus on what's truly relevant.

Be specific with details

Details help AI provide responses that match your exact needs. Specifics like word count, tone (formal or friendly), or even the type of information you want (such as bullet points) can make responses more tailored to your request.

Example

Instead of 'Describe Italy', try 'Give me a short description of Italy's top tourist attractions, in under 100 words'.

Use step by step instructions for complex tasks

When you need AI to handle a multi-part task, it's helpful to break down instructions into steps. This way, AI can follow each part of the instruction more accurately.

Example

If you need a summary and analysis, ask it in steps: 'First, summarize the main points of this article. Then, analyse its pros and cons.'

This clear structure helps AI handle each part without mixing up the information.

Experiment and refine

AI responds differently to slight changes in wording, so don't be afraid to experiment. If the response isn't what you were expecting, try rephrasing the prompt or adding more details. Sometimes, minor tweaks can lead to major improvements.

Example

If 'List the health benefits of exercising' gives you too general a response, try 'List five surprising health benefits of exercising regularly'.

By refining the prompt, you can make the response even more relevant and focused.

Challenge responses

If you do not get an effective response, or simply disagree with the answer, don't hesitate to let it know about what you do not like.

Example

If you get an incomplete response, simply reply with 'That is not what I asked for, try again.'

Techniques for effective prompt engineering

Role-playing prompts

Role-playing prompts involve assigning a 'role' to AI, which helps it adopt a specific perspective. For example, if you want marketing advice, you can ask AI to act as a 'marketing expert'.

Example

You are a nutritionist. Create a meal plan for someone who wants to lose weight but can't eat gluten.

This prompt helps AI respond more like an expert in the chosen field, giving more specialized advice.

Questioning prompts

Asking questions within a prompt can make AI generate deeper and more thoughtful responses. Questions also encourage AI to address specific aspects, which can lead to more informative answers.

Example

What are the main benefits of electric cars over traditional gas-powered cars? List at least three.

AI will focus on the comparison, giving a detailed answer based on the question.

Constraint-based prompts

Constraints are limits you set in the prompt, such as word count or format. This is especially useful if you need a summary or specific format, as it helps AI shape its response to fit your needs.

Example

Explain photosynthesis in 50 words or less.

This constraint keeps the response short and to the point.

Comparison prompts

Comparison prompts work well when you want AI to evaluate two or more options. This is particularly helpful for making decisions or understanding pros and cons.

Example

Compare the advantages of working from home versus working from an office. Include at least two points for each.

This prompt will give a structured response that's easy to evaluate.

Narrative or creative prompts

For creative tasks, like story writing or ideation, prompts can encourage AI to think in a more imaginative way. These are great for writers or anyone in creative fields.

Example

Write a short story about a child who discovers a magical library.

AI will respond creatively, following the narrative direction set by the prompt.

Context-appropriate prompts

For simple explanations, give it context for the situation.

Example

Explain subdivision to a nine-year-old; assume that they are struggling with maths.

Practical applications of prompt engineering

Prompt engineering can be applied across various roles and everyday tasks. Here are some real-world examples:

For work: Creating professional emails

Example

Write a polite follow-up email to a client reminding them of the upcoming deadline for submitting feedback.

This prompt is precise, and AI can deliver a draft that is professional and respectful.

For students: Simplifying complex topics

Example

Explain the main events of the American Revolution in simple language for a high school history assignment.

By specifying the level of detail and audience, AI will provide an appropriate answer for educational purposes.

For everyday use: Making a grocery list

Example

Create a grocery list for making a week's worth of healthy dinners. Include items needed for simple recipes.

This practical use of prompts saves time and helps users plan efficiently.

For difficult conversations: Write a termination letter

Example

Write a letter to my Technical Adviser, who has not been performing well enough over the past few months, letting them know that I no longer require their services. Be kind and grateful for their contributions.

2

Case Study

How prompt engineering helped Naamya organize her work

Naamya, a freelance graphic designer, often struggled to stay organized and brainstorm new ideas. Here's how she used prompt engineering to simplify her tasks:

1. **Time management**: She asked, 'Create a daily schedule for a freelancer balancing three client projects, personal work and learning time.' AI provided a detailed, organized schedule that kept her on track.

2. **Brainstorming ideas**: For a client project, she prompted the AI: 'Suggest five logo concepts for an eco-friendly brand targeting young adults.' AI's ideas helped her develop a creative direction faster.

3. **Client communication**: Naamya needed to update a client on her progress. She used the prompt, 'Write a brief, friendly project update for a client, explaining that the design is on track and will be ready by the agreed deadline.' AI produced a professional message that saved her time drafting emails.

4. **Design iterations**: Naamya got stuck on ideas for a logo for a particular brand. She used an AI software that can generate images and asked for 10 iterations, describing the brand look and feel, colours and iconography. She used the prompt 'You are a logo designer, creating a new logo for a construction company that values quality and speed of work. Its colours

are red and black and the logo needs to instil a sense of trust with big corporate clients'.

With these prompts, Naamya discovered how prompt engineering could make her workday smoother, more productive and less stressful.

Conclusion

Prompt engineering is a powerful way to make AI work for you. By learning a few basic techniques, anyone can improve the quality of responses they get from AI, whether they're drafting an email, learning a new topic or planning a project. The key elements—clarity, context, specificity, structure and iteration—help you create prompts that yield meaningful and useful answers.

You're now equipped to start using prompt engineering in your daily life. Remember, practice makes perfect. The more you experiment and refine, the better you'll get at crafting prompts that give you exactly the results you need.

3

Advanced Techniques in AI Prompt Engineering

BEYOND BASIC PROMPTING, ADVANCED TECHNIQUES can help us achieve nuanced, accurate and insightful responses from AI for tasks of varying complexity.

In this chapter, we'll explore a range of advanced prompt engineering techniques, illustrated with examples relevant to the Indian context. Whether you're drafting emails, solving complex problems or brainstorming ideas, these techniques will enable you to make the most of AI's capabilities.

Key techniques for effective prompt engineering

1. Zero-shot prompting

Zero-shot prompting involves asking AI to perform a task directly, without providing any examples or background information. This technique relies on the model's general knowledge to deliver a response. It's often used for straightforward questions where specialized knowledge or examples aren't necessary.

Example

List three benefits of yoga for mental health.

AI would generate an answer based on general knowledge about yoga's mental health benefits, such as stress reduction, improved focus and relaxation, without needing additional context.

When to use: Use zero-shot prompting for general questions or tasks that don't require specific examples or context.

2. Few-shot prompting

Few-shot prompting involves giving AI a few examples before asking it to respond. This is useful when the prompt needs to clarify the response's tone, style or structure. By providing similar examples, you guide AI to produce responses that match the desired pattern.

Example

Here's how we write restaurant reviews

1. Gulati's in Delhi: A perfect place for North Indian cuisine. The butter chicken is a must-try!
2. Chokhi Dhani in Jaipur: A delightful experience with traditional Rajasthani food and cultural activities.

Now write a review for a popular South Indian restaurant in Bangalore.

AI would mimic the example format, giving a review that's concise, focused and descriptive.

When to use: Use few-shot prompting for tasks where style, tone or format is important, such as creating reviews, summaries or structured content.

3. Chain-of-thought prompting

Chain-of-thought prompting encourages AI to think through each step of a problem before giving a final answer. This is especially useful for complex tasks that require reasoning, logical steps or calculations.

Example

I need to calculate the total price of a family outing. Ticket prices are ₹500 each for two adults and ₹300 each for two children.

First, calculate the cost for adults, then for children, and finally add them.

AI would go through each step: calculating the total for adults (₹1,000), then for children (₹600), and summing them to give a final answer (₹1,600).

When to use: Chain-of-thought prompting is ideal for tasks that involve multiple steps or logical reasoning, such as budgeting, travel planning or solving maths problems.

4. Meta prompting

Meta prompting is a technique where you ask AI to generate other prompts. This approach is useful for discovering various ways to approach a task, generating ideas or exploring different methods of asking questions.

Example

Create three different prompts that could help someone brainstorm ideas for a blog post on the benefits of Ayurveda in daily life.

AI might suggest prompts such as:

1. Explain how Ayurveda can help manage stress naturally.
2. List simple Ayurvedic practices for a healthier lifestyle.
3. Discuss the benefits of Ayurvedic herbs commonly found in Indian households.

When to use: Use meta prompting when you need to generate multiple variations of a prompt or explore different ways of approaching a topic.

5. Self-consistency

Self-consistency involves asking AI to produce multiple answers to a question, then choosing the most consistent response. This technique is useful for improving accuracy and reliability, especially for complex tasks.

Example

What are the top three historical sites to visit in Delhi?

AI might give numerous responses like the Red Fort, Qutub Minar and India Gate. By generating multiple responses and comparing them, you can confirm consistency in AI's recommendations.

When to use: Self-consistency is valuable for tasks where accuracy is critical, such as fact-finding or recommendation lists.

6. Generate knowledge prompting

This involves asking AI to generate relevant background information before it answers a question. This helps ensure AI's response is informed and contextualized.

Example

Before explaining the benefits of organic farming, provide a brief overview of the current state of agriculture in India.

This approach encourages AI to first generate relevant context, making its response on organic farming more meaningful.

When to use: Use generate knowledge prompting when the answer depends on a foundational understanding of a broader topic.

7. Prompt chaining

Prompt chaining links multiple prompts together, with each prompt building on the previous one's response. This technique helps in managing complex tasks in stages, where each step informs the next.

Example

1. List the main ingredients of a traditional Hyderabadi biryani.
2. Explain how each ingredient contributes to the overall flavour of the biryani.

3. Provide a step by step guide for preparing Hyderabadi biryani.

Each response informs the following step, resulting in a cohesive output.

When to use: Use prompt chaining for tasks that require building information gradually, such as tutorials or step by step explanations.

8. Tree of thoughts

Tree of thoughts explores multiple paths or reasoning steps before arriving at a conclusion. This technique allows AI to consider different perspectives or approaches, particularly useful for brainstorming or problem-solving.

Example

Suggest three different strategies for improving water conservation in Indian cities.

AI might provide three distinct ideas, such as rainwater harvesting, awareness campaigns and urban green spaces, each as separate 'branches' of thought.

When to use: Use tree of thoughts when exploring various solutions or brainstorming ideas or looking at different viewpoints.

9. Retrieval augmented generation

Retrieval augmented generation integrates external information into AI's response. This allows the model to reference updated or specialized data, enhancing the relevance of its answers.

Example

Using recent government reports, explain the current challenges facing the Indian education system.

This prompt would require AI to pull in relevant and recent information to provide an accurate response.

When to use: Use retrieval augmented generation when you need information that may not be included in AI's base knowledge, like recent events or specific statistics.

10. Reflexion

Reflexion prompts encourage AI to reflect on its own previous answers. This can lead to more refined, accurate responses by allowing the model to identify and correct any mistakes.

Example

Explain the major festivals celebrated in India. Now, review your answer and add any key festivals you may have missed.

AI reflects on its response, ensuring completeness and accuracy.

When to use: Reflexion is useful for tasks where a comprehensive answer is required and where missed details could be critical.

Conclusion

Advanced prompt engineering techniques provide powerful ways to interact with AI, helping you achieve precise, insightful and contextually rich responses. Whether you need to ask AI to think through a problem step by step, compare options, generate background knowledge or reflect on its previous answers, these techniques open up new possibilities for getting the most out of AI.

From zero-shot prompting for quick tasks to retrieval-augmented generation for data-driven inquiries, these methods give you a versatile toolkit. As you apply these techniques, you'll find that AI can become a more effective partner in your everyday life, from professional tasks to personal projects. Experimenting with different techniques will empower you to tailor AI's responses to suit your exact needs, making AI a useful and reliable tool for virtually any scenario.

4

Prompt Engineering Techniques

IN TODAY'S FAST-PACED WORLD, A wide range of skills is essential to thrive personally and professionally. This chapter brings together a comprehensive selection of categories and roles that span various domains—from leadership and innovation to wellness and personal growth.

Each category is thoughtfully crafted to address key areas of expertise, providing practical insights and structured prompts for professionals, mentors and service providers to excel in their fields. Whether it's helping a client set realistic goals, supporting a team through operational challenges, or offering guidance in creative expression, these roles contribute to a more connected, effective and resilient society.

The prompts and advanced techniques featured here are tailored to empower professionals by incorporating industry best practices, culturally relevant approaches and a commitment to continuous growth. By embracing these diverse prompts, individuals will be better equipped to understand and respond to the unique needs they have.

We will see how different roles work in harmony to support growth and excellence across multiple aspects of life and work. The prompts presented for each role are designed not only to inspire action but also to encourage a reflective, purposeful approach to service and personal development. By drawing upon this wide array of skills and strategies, individuals can enhance their capacity to lead, create, nurture and transform.

This chapter serves as a resource and a reminder that, through intentional practice, we can all become better mentors, leaders, creatives and caregivers, building a future that is both impactful and fulfilling.

Here is a list of categories and roles in each category.

Category	Role
Leadership, Strategy and Management	Business Leader, Team Manager, Chief Executive Officer (CEO), Chief Technology Officer (CTO), Project Manager, Operations Manager, Department Head, Strategy Consultant, Board Member
Start-up, Entrepreneurship and Innovation	Entrepreneur, Start-up Founder, Venture Capitalist, Innovation Strategist
Technology, Development and IT	Software Developer, AI/Machine Learning (ML) Engineer, DevOps Engineer, IT Manager, Cybersecurity Specialist, User Experience (UX)/User Interface (UI) Designer, Mobile App Developer
Sales, Marketing and Communications	Sales Executive, Marketing Professional, Real Estate Agent, Travel Agent, Advertising Manager
Legal, Government and Policy	Advocate (Lawyer), Government Officer, Politician, Legal Consultant, Policy Advisor, Regulatory Affairs Manager
Finance, Accounting and Risk Management	Financial Analyst, Accountant, Risk Manager, Tax Consultant, Internal Auditor, Financial Controller
Education, Research and Mentorship	Teacher, Educational Administrator, Researcher, Mentor, Academic Counsellor, Curriculum Developer

Health, Wellness and Caregiving	Doctor, Nutritionist, Physiotherapist, Mental Health Counsellor
Creative Arts, Design and Media	Graphic Designer, Content Writer, Video Editor, Social Media Manager
Human Resources (HR), Training and Development	HR Manager, Recruitment Specialist, Training and Development Specialist, Employee Relations Specialist
Operations, Supply Chain and Logistics	Supply Chain Manager, Operations Manager, Logistics Coordinator
Wellness, Personal Growth and Lifestyle	Life Coach, Meditation Trainer, Yoga Trainer

5

Leadership, Strategy and Management Prompts

Leadership and management roles are key to steering an organization towards success. These roles require a combination of strategic vision and problem-solving and effective communication skills to ensure organizational growth, innovation and team cohesion.

∞

Role 1: Business Leader

A Business Leader is responsible for setting the strategic direction of a company. They must balance growth, innovation and profitability while making high-stakes decisions that impact the entire organization.

◆

Context

The company, a mid-sized manufacturer of personal care products, is considering diversifying into the eco-friendly home cleaning market. This sector is growing but competitive. The company has the necessary capital but must be cautious about liquidity and resource allocation.

Prompt 1: Strategic decision-making

I need to decide whether to invest in a new product line. Please provide a pros and cons analysis.

Sample output

Pros: Expands customer base, potential for increased revenue, strengthens market position

Cons: Requires significant capital investment, potential for market saturation, longer time to profitability.

Tip for customizing: Tailor the product line details to a specific industry or market.

◆

Context

A software development firm with 200 employees has noted declining engagement in sales and customer support. The firm operates a strict 9–5 schedule with limited team interactions and lacks a formal recognition system.

Prompt 2: Team engagement

How can I boost employee engagement across all departments?

Sample output

1. Introduce flexible work hours to improve work–life balance.
2. Hold regular team-building activities to foster collaboration.
3. Create a recognition programme to celebrate achievements.

Tip for customizing: Adjust based on the company culture and size.

Advanced prompt

You are a star product manager. Help me decide whether and how much to invest in a new product line. Size up and provide your rationale for the TAM, SAM and SOM[2], and provide a critical

---

[2] Total Addressable Market, Serviceable Addressable Market and Serviceable Obtainable Market

analysis of the market opportunity. List the pros and cons. Cite your sources.

◆

Context

The company is a technology start-up in its growth phase, focusing on expanding its product range and entering new markets. It has experienced variable revenue trends due to fluctuating market demands and economic conditions. The leadership is planning for strategic investments in research and development (R&D) and marketing to boost competitiveness.

Prompt 3: Financial planning

What factors should I consider when creating a financial plan for the next fiscal year?

Sample output

1. Review current revenue trends and forecast future growth.
2. Allocate funds to key areas like R&D, marketing and HR.
3. Consider external economic factors that could impact profitability.

Tip for customizing: Focus on specific areas such as budget cuts or aggressive growth plans.

Advanced prompt

Act as an expert chief financial officer (CFO) in the [industry name] industry. My company is at the [stage of the company] stage with an approximate annual revenue of [value in ₹]. Begin by asking me a series of questions to gather detailed information needed to build up my company's financials. After collecting the necessary data, analyse the company's current financial situation and guide me through additional questions to help define the company's goals for the next fiscal year. Using this information, develop a comprehensive financial plan for the upcoming fiscal year. From this plan, derive specific hiring strategies, training programmes, and set measurable quarterly sales targets to ensure we meet or exceed our overall objectives.

$$\infty$$

Role 2: Team Manager

A Team Manager oversees daily team operations and ensures that goals are met. They resolve conflicts, delegate tasks and foster a collaborative environment to maintain productivity.

◆

Context

The company operates a small customer service team where two key members are in disagreement, which is affecting their work. The team is tightly knit and any visible conflict could potentially disrupt overall morale. The team leader is seeking ways to address the issue discreetly and effectively.

Prompt 1: Conflict resolution

How can I resolve a conflict between two team members without affecting overall morale?

Sample output

1. Arrange a private meeting with both individuals to understand their perspectives.
2. Mediate the conversation and encourage them to find a mutually beneficial solution.
3. Set clear guidelines for future collaboration.

Tip for customizing: Modify based on the severity of the conflict or team dynamics.

Advanced prompt

I have two team members in conflict within a team of [x] members, which is part of a larger organization with [y] members.

- **Colleague 1**: [Name], [age], [gender], [relationship status], with a LinkedIn profile at [link].
- **Colleague 2**: [Name], [age], [gender], [relationship status], with a LinkedIn profile at [link].

Analyse any relevant data from their LinkedIn profiles to understand their professional backgrounds, roles and potential strengths. Use this information to suggest strategies to resolve the conflict effectively while maintaining or enhancing overall team morale. Ensure that the resolution fosters collaboration and aligns with the larger organizational goals.[3]

◆

Context

The project team is working on a high-priority software development project with tight deadlines. The team consists of diverse talents, including developers, designers and quality assurance (QA) specialists. Efficient task delegation is crucial to meet project timelines while ensuring high-quality outputs. The project manager aims to leverage individual strengths to maximize productivity.

Prompt 2: Task delegation

What are the best practices for delegating tasks efficiently in a fast-paced project?

---

[3]Note that not all tools have real-time access to the internet. Moreover, the prompt assumes you've already shared the organizational goals with the tool.

Sample output

1. Assign tasks based on individual strengths and expertise.
2. Set clear deadlines and provide necessary resources.
3. Monitor progress through regular check-ins without micromanaging.

Tip for customizing: Adjust based on team size and the complexity of the project.

Advanced prompt

1. As a Team Manager in a fast-paced environment I need to ensure tasks are delegated efficiently to achieve project goals without compromising quality or team morale. My team comprises individuals with diverse skills, work styles and availability, including remote and in-office members. I seek best practices for assessing team strengths, prioritizing high-impact tasks, breaking down complex deliverables and fostering collaboration across diverse working styles. Additionally, I need strategies for clear communication and real-time task tracking and empowering team members to take ownership while maintaining transparency and accountability. Guidance on performance monitoring, constructive feedback and refining delegation processes over time is essential to ensure continuous improvement, adaptability and overall success in a high-pressure project environment.

2. Create a detailed project plan and assign tasks to my team based on their individual strengths and weaknesses. I have a team of [number of members] with varying skills: for example, [Name] is strong in [strengths like coding or design] but has weaknesses in [weak areas like time management or attention to detail]. Consider each member's current workload and availability, so tasks are balanced without overloading anyone. The project goals include [briefly mention goals, like meeting specific deadlines or quality benchmarks], with key milestones

to be met by [timeline or phase deadlines]. Ensure that tasks are prioritized as high, medium or low and that timelines are realistic, with regular progress checkpoints [weekly or bi-weekly] to stay on track. Adjust assignments in real time if needed; for example, if a team member completes a task early or falls behind; and make any necessary changes as the project evolves. The final output should be a dynamic project plan that keeps workloads balanced, leverages individual skill sets and maintains accountability.

◆

Context

The team includes a recently hired developer who is struggling to meet performance standards in a fast-paced tech company. The Team Manager wants to address the issue constructively to enhance the developer's productivity and integration into the team without causing discouragement.

Prompt 3: Performance feedback

How can I give constructive feedback to a team member who is underperforming?

Sample output

1. Focus on specific behaviours rather than personal traits.
2. Provide actionable suggestions for improvement.
3. Offer support and resources to help them succeed.

Tip for customizing: Include specific examples of performance issues to give clearer feedback.

Advanced prompt

You are analysing team performance data from JIRA over the last six months. Begin by extracting metadata from the attached JIRA snapshot, including metrics for each team member's bugs, on-time delivery track record and comments. Use this data to compare the metrics of an individual team member against the team average. Create visualizations to show their metrics on a bell curve, with separate charts for each measure. Summarize the findings in a one-page report, highlighting performance strengths and areas for improvement. For each improvement area, provide three specific strategies to enhance their performance in terms of bug reduction, timeliness and collaboration.

Role 3: Chief Executive Officer

The CEO is the highest-ranking executive in a company, responsible for overall strategic decisions. They guide the company towards growth while maintaining alignment with its vision and goals.

◆

Context

The company is a mid-sized renewable energy firm looking to solidify its position in an evolving market characterized by rapid technological advancements and shifting regulatory landscapes. Leaders aim to craft a strategy that not only supports steady growth but also adapts to unexpected changes in the environment.

Prompt 1: Long-term strategy

How can I develop a long-term strategy that ensures sustainable growth for the next five years?

Sample output

1. Analyse current market trends and emerging technologies.
2. Set clear objectives that align with the company's vision.
3. Create a flexible plan that allows for adjustments based on market conditions.

Tip for customizing: Adjust based on the company's industry and market position.

◆

Context

The company, a large food production entity, has encountered a supply chain disruption affecting major products. The management needs to inform stakeholders, including suppliers, customers and investors, about the situation and the measures being implemented to mitigate its impact.

Prompt 2: Crisis communication

What's the best approach for communicating a crisis situation to stakeholders?

Sample output

1. Be transparent about the situation and provide clear facts.
2. Explain the steps the company is taking to resolve the issue.
3. Reassure stakeholders with a plan for recovery from the crisis and future prevention strategies.

Tip for customizing: Include specific scenarios, such as product recalls or financial crises.

Advanced prompt

Imagine you are the acting CEO of [your company name], currently navigating a crisis—[brief description of the situation]. Identify the key stakeholders you should prioritize communicating with, the optimal frequency and timing of messages (message cadence), and the most effective formats for delivering these communications (e.g., email, meetings, press releases). For each stakeholder group, outline the critical points that must be addressed and recommend the appropriate tone (e.g., empathetic, reassuring, authoritative) to ensure clarity, trust and alignment during this challenging time.

◆

Context

The organization is a burgeoning tech start-up aiming to scale operations and enter new markets. To drive this growth, it's essential to attract experienced leaders who can bring fresh insights and strategies. The company is focused on building a reputation as an innovator in its field to appeal to top industry talent.

Prompt 3: Talent acquisition

How can I attract top talent to key leadership positions in my organization?

Sample output

1. Highlight the company's growth potential and mission.
2. Offer competitive compensation packages with benefits that appeal to senior-level candidates.
3. Foster a culture of innovation and leadership development.

Tip for customizing: Adjust the strategy based on company size and industry.

Advanced prompt

I am seeking actionable strategies to attract top-tier talent for key leadership positions in my organization. The focus is on building a leadership team that aligns with our company culture, drives innovation and accelerates growth. Consider the following factors in your response:

1. **Employer branding**

    » How can I position my organization as an employer of choice for leaders in our industry?

» What specific branding initiatives or messaging can highlight our company's mission, values and growth opportunities to appeal to top talent?

2. Compensation and benefits

» What are the latest trends in competitive compensation packages for leadership roles, including financial and non-financial incentives?

» How can I structure benefits to attract experienced and visionary leaders without straining organizational resources?

3. Talent identification and outreach

» How can I identify high-potential candidates, both active and passive, who align with the skills and experience we need?

» What outreach strategies, including executive search firms, networking and social platforms, are most effective for engaging with top talent?

4. Selection process

» What best practices can I follow to create a rigorous yet attractive recruitment process for leadership roles?

» How can I assess not just qualifications but cultural fit, adaptability and strategic vision during the interview and evaluation process?

5. Retention and onboarding

» How can I ensure that once hired, leaders feel valued and supported to succeed in their roles?

» What onboarding and ongoing development programmes should I implement to retain leadership talent and foster long-term engagement?

Provide detailed, step by step recommendations, including examples from successful companies, tools or platforms to leverage, and measurable key performance indicators (KPIs), to track progress. Additionally, consider how the strategies might differ for attracting leadership talent in industries that are highly competitive, niche or undergoing rapid transformation.

Role 4: Chief Technology Officer

The CTO oversees the company's technology strategy and ensures that technological initiatives align with business goals. They manage innovation, infrastructure and the integration of new technologies.

◆

Context

The company is a mid-sized e-commerce platform aiming to enhance its user experience and operational efficiency through technology. As it plans for expansion in both market reach and product offerings, the leadership seeks to align its technological capabilities with these growth objectives over the next three years.

Prompt 1: Technology road map

How can I create a three year technology road map that aligns with the company's growth?

Sample output

1. Identify key business goals and map out technology requirements to support them.

2. Prioritize projects based on their potential impact and resource availability.

3. Include plans for upskilling the tech team and adopting emerging technologies.

Tip for customizing: Focus on specific areas such as software development, cloud infrastructure, data analytics.

Advanced prompt

I am seeking guidance on creating a three-year technology road map that aligns with my company's growth objectives and drives innovation, efficiency and scalability. Consider the following key aspects in your response:

1. **Strategic alignment**

    »   How can I align the technology road map with the company's long-term goals, market trends and competitive landscape?

    »   What steps should I take to ensure that the road map supports both revenue growth and operational excellence?

2. **Assessment of current capabilities**

    »   What frameworks can I use to evaluate our current technology stack, identify gaps and prioritize upgrades or replacements?

    »   How can I assess team capabilities and ensure alignment between the road map and internal technical expertise?

3. **Prioritization of initiatives**

    »   How do I prioritize technology initiatives across categories like infrastructure, software development, cybersecurity, data analytics and automation?

» What factors, such as return on investment (ROI), customer impact or competitive advantage, should guide the prioritization process?

4. Stakeholder engagement

» How can I involve key stakeholders from various departments to ensure the road map reflects cross-functional needs and buy-in?

» What communication strategies will best convey the road map to both technical and non-technical stakeholders?

5. Resource allocation

» How should I budget for technology investments over the next three years to balance immediate needs with future growth?

» What are the best practices for securing leadership approval and funding for major technology initiatives?

6. Implementation and flexibility

» How can I ensure that the road map is actionable, with clear milestones, timelines and accountability, for each initiative?

» What strategies can I use to maintain flexibility and adapt the road map to evolving business needs and emerging technologies?

7. Metrics and success criteria

» What KPIs should I track to measure the success of the technology road map and its impact on business outcomes?

» How do I establish feedback loops to continuously improve the road map based on results and stakeholder input?

Provide a detailed, step by step guide to creating and implementing a three-year technology road map. Include frameworks, tools or methodologies that can assist in planning and execution, as well as examples from successful organizations. Ensure the response covers both strategic and operational perspectives, enabling my company to achieve sustainable growth through effective technology planning.

◆

Context

The company is a financial services provider handling sensitive client data, requiring stringent security measures against cyberthreats. With increasing online transactions, the firm aims to establish a robust cybersecurity framework to safeguard its assets and client information.

Prompt 2: Cybersecurity plan

What steps should I take to build a strong cybersecurity framework?

Sample output

1. Conduct a risk assessment to identify vulnerabilities.
2. Implement firewalls, encryption and multi-factor authentication.
3. Regularly update systems and conduct employee training on security protocols.

Tip for customizing: Adjust the focus based on the company's size or industry (e.g., fintech, healthcare).

Advanced prompt

You are a cybersecurity implementation expert advising an e-commerce start-up. Develop a list of the top 10 cybersecurity measures to implement, ranked in ascending order of cost and descending order of impact. For each recommendation, explain its security value, approximate cost level and how it mitigates specific threats. Cover a range of areas, including employee training, network security, data encryption, access control and incident response, with a focus on high-impact, budget-friendly options for start-ups.

◆

Context

The company is a software development firm looking to maintain its competitive edge in a rapidly evolving tech industry. The leadership seeks to cultivate an environment that not only values but actively promotes innovation among its technical staff to spur ongoing advancements and breakthroughs.

Prompt 3: Managing innovation

How can I foster a culture of innovation within the tech department?

Sample output

1. Encourage experimentation by allocating resources for R&D projects.
2. Hold hackathons or innovation challenges to stimulate creative solutions.
3. Offer incentives for successful innovative ideas that impact the business.

Tip for customizing: Customize based on the scale of innovation and the industry.

Advanced prompt

As the CTO of a company in the [industry], you are aiming to foster a culture of innovation within your tech department of [x] team members. Considering your budget constraints, start with foundational questions about your team's structure, current practices and budget allocations. Next, clarify the primary goals for innovation and evaluate feasible initiatives. Based on responses, arrive at the top three achievable ideas that will foster innovation, create engagement and align with your department's capabilities.

∞

Role 5: Project Manager

A Project Manager is responsible for planning, executing and completing projects within deadlines and budgets. They coordinate teams, manage resources and ensure that project goals are met.

◆

Context

The company is a start-up specializing in consumer electronics, preparing to launch its first smart home device. To ensure a successful market entry, the project team needs a detailed plan that covers all aspects from development to distribution, while managing limited resources and tight deadlines.

Prompt 1: Project planning

How can I create a project plan for launching a new product?

Sample output

1. Define the project scope and key milestones.
2. Create a timeline with specific deliverables for each phase.
3. Assign tasks and resources while identifying potential risks.

Tip for customizing: Adjust based on the complexity and timeline of the project.

Advanced prompt

I am the project manager for [project name]. This product is designed for [target market], aiming to deliver [product benefits]. Our team consists of [x] members: [aa] developers, [bb] testers and [cc] in roles such as [other roles]. I've attached the architecture diagram and technical specification documents for reference.

Using this information, please provide the following:

1. **Work breakdown structure (WBS):** Develop a detailed WBS that decomposes the project into phases, deliverables and tasks, specifying dependencies, prerequisites and a clear hierarchy.
2. **Estimation:** Provide both low and high estimates (in hours) for each task, taking into account potential complexities, risks and resource availability.
3. **Timeline and Gantt chart:** Map the project on to a Gantt chart, showing task durations, milestones, dependencies and any overlapping or parallel tasks to optimize project flow. Include expected start and end dates based on the estimates.
4. **Resource allocation:** Assign tasks to team members, factoring in their roles, expertise and capacity. Account for potential constraints, such as leave, skill overlap and task-specific expertise, to optimize task distribution.
5. **Project plan and budget:** Create a comprehensive project plan document, outlining goals, scope, deliverables, timelines and responsibilities. Include a detailed budget, accounting for personnel costs, potential overtime, software/hardware needs and contingency for unforeseen expenses.
6. **Risk management:** Identify any potential risks or blockers in each phase of the project. Include mitigation strategies, risk ownership and contingency plans, where applicable.
7. **Quality assurance:** Outline QA and testing phases in alignment with the development timeline, including specific tester tasks, code review processes and acceptance criteria.

8. **Reporting and communication:** Establish a reporting schedule with regular progress updates, review points and communication strategies for key stakeholders.

Please ensure that each of these deliverables is precise and actionable, with clear, realistic timelines, and resource distribution is based on the capabilities and roles of team members.

◆

Context

The company is an engineering firm working on a large-scale infrastructure project with significant investments at stake. Due to the complexity and duration of the project, identifying and managing risks is crucial to prevent overruns and ensure project success within the stipulated time frame and budget.

Prompt 2: Risk management

What are the best practices for identifying and mitigating project risks?

Sample output

1. Conduct a risk assessment to identify potential challenges.
2. Create contingency plans for high-risk scenarios.
3. Monitor risks throughout the project life cycle and adjust plans accordingly.

Tip for customizing: Modify based on the industry or type of project (e.g., IT, construction).

◆

Context

The project involves a new software platform development, bringing together specialists from software development, marketing, operations and customer service. Effective collaboration is essential to integrate diverse perspectives and expertise, ensuring the platform meets varied stakeholder requirements and is delivered on schedule.

Prompt 3: Team collaboration

How can I improve collaboration among cross-functional teams working on a large project?

Sample output

1. Establish clear communication channels using tools like Slack or Microsoft Teams.
2. Hold regular check-ins to ensure alignment across teams.
3. Encourage knowledge sharing by promoting open discussions and feedback sessions.

Tip for customizing: Tailor the advice depending on the team structure or remote collaboration needs.

∞

Role 6: Operations Manager

An Operations Manager oversees the day-to-day operations of a company. They focus on optimizing processes, improving efficiency and ensuring smooth workflows across departments.

◆

Context

The company is a medium-sized manufacturer of automotive parts facing increased demand and competition. To meet these challenges and reduce operational costs, leadership is focused on optimizing the production process by identifying inefficiencies and integrating modern automation technologies.

Prompt 1: Process improvement

How can I streamline the production process to improve efficiency?

Sample output

1. Identify bottlenecks in the production line and analyse the root causes.
2. Implement automation tools to reduce manual work.
3. Train employees on new processes and monitor performance improvements.

Tip for customizing: Focus on specific areas like supply chain management and resource allocation.

Advanced prompt

Act as the operations manager in our plant, where we produce [type of product]. Our production metrics by shift are [metric 1], [metric 2] and [metric 3]. Help me identify bottlenecks in our production line by:

1. **Diagnosing bottlenecks**: Ask questions to assess production speed, downtime, labour use, material flow, metric variability, quality control, waste rates and supply chain factors.
2. **Root cause analysis**: Lead a structured root cause analysis (RCA) using techniques like 5 Whys, Fishbone diagrams and FMEA[4]. Investigate issues across machine limits, operator skills, workflow inefficiencies, supply chain delays and environmental factors.
3. **Automation recommendations**: Propose automation tools to reduce manual work and increase efficiency, including solutions for repetitive tasks, real-time monitoring, quality control and inventory management.
4. **Training and implementation manual**: Develop a training

---

[4]Failure Mode and Effect Analysis (FMEA) is a preventive technique that helps identify potential failure modes in a system and their causes and effects.

manual covering new processes, automation tools, updated roles, monitoring guidelines, troubleshooting and KPIs. Include safety protocols, best practices and continuous improvement steps.

Produce a complete training and operations manual that integrates new processes and automation recommendations with a plan to track and sustain performance improvements.

◆

Context

The company is a regional food processing firm that has experienced rising costs in raw materials and energy. To maintain profitability without compromising product quality, the firm is exploring various cost-cutting measures that can be implemented across its operations.

Prompt 2: Cost reduction

What are some strategies to reduce operational costs without affecting quality?

Sample output

1. Negotiate with suppliers to secure better pricing.
2. Optimize inventory management to reduce waste.
3. Implement energy-efficient practices to cut down on utilities.

Tip for customizing: Include specific industries or departments (e.g., manufacturing, logistics).

◆

Context

The company is a multinational corporation with multiple divisions including sales, manufacturing and logistics. It aims to enhance oversight and improve efficiency by implementing a standardized system for measuring and comparing performance across these varied departments.

Prompt 3: Performance tracking

How can I track and measure operational performance across departments?

Sample output

1. Use KPIs such as production rate, lead time and defect rates to monitor performance.
2. Implement dashboards to visualize real-time data.
3. Hold monthly reviews with department heads to assess progress and make adjustments.

Advanced prompt

My company operates in the [industry] with a [company size: revenue, headcount, etc.] and [n] people across [m] departments. Based on this structure, what KPIs can I implement to effectively track and measure operational performance across departments? Additionally, provide a mock dashboard design that aligns these KPIs with the company's growth objectives.

Tip for customizing: Tailor KPIs to different departments based on the company's objectives.

Role 7: Department Head

A Department Head manages a specific division within an organization. They oversee staff, budgets and operations to ensure that departmental goals align with the overall company objectives.

◆

Context

The department is part of a larger financial services company, specializing in customer service. The team has been underperforming due to unclear goals and lack of motivation. The department head is looking for strategies to enhance overall performance, ensure goal alignment and improve employee engagement.

Prompt 1: Team performance

How can I improve team performance within my department?

Sample output

1. Set clear, achievable goals for each team member.
2. Provide regular feedback and coaching to help them reach their targets.
3. Encourage collaboration by fostering a team-oriented culture.

Tip for customizing: Adjust the focus based on the type of department (e.g., sales, HR, marketing).

◆

Context

The department is part of a large educational institution, overseeing campus facilities and maintenance. With fixed annual budget allocations and unexpected repair needs arising frequently, efficient budget management is crucial to ensure all operations continue smoothly without exceeding financial boundaries.

Prompt 2: Budget management

What are the best practices for managing my department's budget efficiently?

Sample output

1. Track spending regularly to ensure that you stay within the budget.
2. Identify areas where you can cut costs without sacrificing quality.
3. Plan for unexpected expenses by creating a contingency fund.

Tip for customizing: Customize based on the size and complexity of the department's operations.

◆

Context

The department is part of a healthcare organization, with roles ranging from administrative staff to healthcare providers. Given the rapid changes in healthcare technology and practices, there is a strong focus on continuous learning and development to keep staff updated and competent, enhancing both employee satisfaction and patient care.

Prompt 3: Employee development

How can I foster employee development within my department?

Sample output

1. Offer professional development programmes that align with both employee and department goals.
2. Encourage mentorship and cross-training to build diverse skills.
3. Provide opportunities for employees to take on leadership roles in projects.

Advanced prompt

I lead a team of [x] members in the [y] department within a [company stage] company operating in the [market/industry]. While we already provide benefits like [tuition reimbursement], [conference expenses], and more, what are three simple and effective strategies to further promote employee development within my department?

Tip for customizing: Adjust based on the skill gaps and needs of the department.

Role 8: Strategy Consultant

A Strategy Consultant advises organizations on their long-term plans and strategies. They help companies in identifying opportunities for growth, streamlining operations and improving overall performance.

Context

The consulting firm specializes in helping retail businesses optimize their operations and increase profitability. Before developing tailored solutions, the firm needs to deeply understand each client's unique situation, market position and strategic goals, ensuring that proposed changes align closely with the client's needs and expectations.

Prompt 1: Client needs analysis

How can I assess a client's needs before proposing a strategic solution?

Sample output

1. Conduct a thorough analysis of the client's business, including financial and market performance.
2. Hold interviews with key stakeholders to understand their goals.
3. Identify gaps in current operations so that productivity can be optimized.

Tip for customizing: Focus on specific industries like retail, tech and finance.

◆

Context

The marketing agency is tasked with aiding a client in the consumer electronics sector to outpace competitors. The agency needs to conduct a detailed competitive analysis to understand market dynamics and develop strategies that leverage the client's unique strengths and address industry challenges.

Prompt 2: Competitive analysis

What are the best practices for conducting a competitive analysis for a client?

Sample output

1. Research the client's top competitors and their market positioning.
2. Identify key strengths and weaknesses in the client's strategy compared to their competitors'.
3. Provide actionable insights to help the client gain a competitive edge.

Tip for customizing: Customize based on the client's industry or market.

◆

Context

The client is a medium-sized software company specializing in cloud-based solutions. With the goal of expanding its market reach and enhancing its technological capabilities, the company is seeking strategies that will enable sustained growth, considering both organic development and potential strategic partnerships.

Prompt 3: Growth strategy

What are some strategies to help a client achieve sustained growth over the next three years?

Sample output

1. Diversify product offerings to cater to new markets.
2. Invest in digital transformation to increase operational efficiency.
3. Explore mergers and acquisitions to expand market share.

Tip for customizing: Adjust based on the size of the client's business and their growth goals.

Role 9: Board Member

A Board Member plays a key role in guiding the strategic direction of an organization. They offer oversight, advise on major decisions and ensure the organization adheres to its mission and long-term goals.

◆

Context

The individual is a new board member of a non-profit organization that provides educational services. The organization has faced recent scrutiny over financial mismanagement. To restore trust and improve operations, the board member aims to enhance governance practices and oversight mechanisms.

Prompt 1: Governance oversight

How can I improve governance and oversight as a board member?

Sample output

1. Ensure that clear governance policies are in place and regularly reviewed.
2. Hold regular meetings to discuss company performance and strategic direction.
3. Ensure transparency and accountability by reviewing key performance metrics.

Tip for customizing: Adjust based on the size and structure of the organization.

◆

Context

The individual serves as a board member for a consumer goods company facing intense competition and market saturation. With emerging trends and shifting consumer preferences, strategic input is crucial to help the company adapt its business model and identify potential growth opportunities in the dynamic market landscape.

Prompt 2: Strategic input

How can I provide strategic input to help the company navigate a challenging market environment?

Sample output

1. Analyse market trends and economic data to forecast challenges.

2. Offer guidance on adapting business models or entering new markets.
3. Encourage investment in innovation and efficiency to stay competitive.

Tip for customizing: Focus on specific market challenges, such as regulation changes and emerging competitors.

◆

Context

A large financial institution deals with a high volume of transactions and extensive regulatory requirements. Given the critical need for robust risk management to protect the institution's assets and reputation, the board is focused on overseeing and continually improving the organization's risk management practices.

Prompt 3: Risk management

What are the best practices for overseeing risk management at the board level?

Sample output

1. Ensure that a comprehensive risk management framework is in place.
2. Regularly review potential risks, including financial, operational and reputational risks.
3. Monitor the effectiveness of risk mitigation strategies and adjust as needed.

Tip for customizing: Tailor the advice based on the type of risks most relevant to the organization.

6

Start-up, Entrepreneurship and Innovation Prompts

Start-up roles require a balance of innovation, risk management and strategic planning. These roles focus on developing new ideas, attracting investors and ensuring sustainable growth in a highly competitive market.

Role 1: Entrepreneur

An Entrepreneur turns ideas into reality by identifying market opportunities, building a team and taking calculated risks to grow the business.

Context

The start-up is a tech company developing SaaS (software-as-a-service) solutions for small and medium businesses (SMBs). The new business model focuses on transitioning from a subscription-only model to a hybrid model combining subscriptions and usage-based pricing. Before implementation, the founder seeks to evaluate the model's feasibility, scalability and potential market impact.

Prompt 1: Business model evaluation

I want to test a new business model for my start-up. Assume that my company operates in the tech space and serves a B2B market. What are the steps to evaluate the potential success of this model?

Sample output

1. **Identify target customers:** Define your B2B audience and their specific pain points.
2. **Conduct a competitive analysis:** Research existing competitors and their business models.
3. **Evaluate revenue streams:** Estimate potential revenue sources based on customer needs and willingness to pay.
4. **Assess scalability:** Ensure that the model can grow without significant cost increases.
5. **Test assumptions:** Use lean methodologies to test hypotheses with minimal resources.

Tips for customizing

- Specify the tech industry you're operating in (e.g., SaaS, AI solutions).
- Include any budgetary or time constraints to refine the business model evaluation further.

◆

Context

The company is a mid-sized e-commerce platform looking to expand into Southeast Asia, a region with significant growth potential but diverse consumer behaviours and regulatory environments. With a constrained marketing budget of $50,000, the company aims to maximize impact by targeting specific customer segments and leveraging cost-effective digital marketing strategies.

Prompt 2: Market entry strategy

I'm planning to enter a new international market. Assume that I
am limited by a marketing budget of $50,000. What are the steps
I should take to ensure a successful entry?

Sample output

1. **Research local regulations:** Understand any legal and
   compliance requirements for the new market.
2. **Define target demographics:** Pinpoint the market
   segment that aligns with your product or service.
3. **Create a marketing plan:** Allocate your $50,000 budget
   efficiently by focusing on high-impact digital channels.
4. **Build local partnerships:** Collaborate with influencers,
   resellers and distributors who know the local market.
5. **Test product–market fit:** Run small-scale pilot
   programmes before a full launch.

Tips for customizing

- Add specific countries or regions to tailor market research
  recommendations.
- Define what kind of product or service you're launching to
  get a more focused entry plan.

◆

Context

The start-up is a seed-stage health-tech company developing an
AI-powered platform for remote patient monitoring. The founder
is preparing a pitch to secure $1 million in funding from venture
capitalists to accelerate product development, expand the team
and execute initial go-to-market strategies in a rapidly growing
industry.

Prompt 3: Fundraising strategy

I'm preparing to pitch my start-up to venture capitalists. Assume that my start-up is in the seed stage and I'm seeking $1 million in funding. How should I structure my pitch?

Sample output

1. **Present your problem and solution clearly:** Start with a compelling story of the problem you're solving.
2. **Highlight your market opportunity:** Provide data on the size and potential of your target market.
3. **Detail your business model:** Explain how you will generate revenue and your growth strategy.
4. **Showcase your team:** Highlight the skills and experience of your core team members.
5. **Outline your financial projections:** Present realistic financials for the next 3–5 years, showing how the $1 million will be used.

Tips for customizing

- Define whether you're seeking funding for product development, marketing or scaling to get more tailored advice.
- Include your industry (e.g., SaaS, fintech) for more precise feedback.

Role 2: Start-up Founder

A Start-up Founder initiates a business venture, leads the vision, and manages the start-up's growth and strategy, often under resource constraints.

Context

The start-up is a seed-stage SaaS company with limited funding, focused on developing and launching its first product. With only three hires possible, the founder must prioritize roles that directly contribute to product development, acquiring initial customers and ensuring customer satisfaction while keeping non-core functions lean through outsourcing or part-time support.

Prompt 1: Early stage team building

I need to build a core team for my start-up, but I can only afford to hire three people initially. How should I prioritize roles and responsibilities?

Sample output

1. **Focus on essential functions:** Prioritize roles in product development, sales and customer service.
2. **Hire versatile individuals:** Look for candidates who can wear multiple hats and adapt to different roles.
3. **Use freelancers or part-timers:** For less critical functions like marketing, consider contract workers.
4. **Delegate and outsource:** Outsource non-core activities like accounting and IT management to save costs.

Tips for customizing

- Specify the industry to receive suggestions on specialized roles (e.g., AI developer, UI/UX designer).
- Define your start-up's immediate needs (e.g., product launch, customer acquisition) for more specific advice.

◆

Context

The start-up, a direct-to-consumer tech-enabled service provider, has experienced rapid growth, doubling its customer base within six months. However, the existing operational structure is struggling to keep up with the demand, leading to delays and service inefficiencies. The founder seeks to scale operations sustainably while maintaining quality and customer satisfaction.

Prompt 2: Managing growth

Our start-up has grown quickly, but I'm struggling to scale its operations. What steps should I take to manage rapid growth?

Sample output

1. **Standardize processes:** Implement consistent workflows to handle increasing workloads efficiently.
2. **Invest in scalable technology:** Use cloud-based tools and automation to streamline operations.
3. **Hire strategically:** Focus on filling critical positions that support your growth, such as customer support or operations management.
4. **Monitor cash flow:** Keep a close eye on finances to ensure that rapid growth doesn't drain resources.

Tips for customizing

- Specify areas of growth (e.g., product demand, customer base) to get tailored operational advice.
- Define whether the challenge is hiring, technology or the supply chain for more focused guidance.

Role 3: Venture Capitalist

A Venture Capitalist invests in early-stage start-ups, offering funding in exchange for equity. They assess the potential for growth and profitability while guiding the founders towards success.

♦

Context

The investor is evaluating a Series A fintech start-up specializing in payment solutions for small businesses. The start-up has shown promising early traction but operates in a highly competitive market. The investor seeks to ensure that the company has strong leadership, a scalable business model, and a clear path to profitability and exit potential before committing $5 million.

Prompt 1: Investment decision

I'm considering investing in a fintech start-up. Assume they're at the Series A stage and seeking $5 million. What key factors should I analyse before making my decision?

Sample output

1. **Evaluate the team:** Ensure the founders have the right experience and skills for scaling the business.
2. **Assess market potential:** Determine the size and growth potential of the fintech market they are targeting.
3. **Review financial health:** Analyse the start-up's current financials, including revenue growth, burn rate and cash flow.
4. **Consider the competitive landscape:** Identify existing competitors and the start-up's differentiation.
5. **Check exit potential:** Ensure the company has a realistic path to exit, whether through acquisition or initial public offering (IPO).

Tips for customizing

- Focus on specific fintech segments (e.g., payments, lending) to get more targeted investment advice.
- Define what kind of returns or time horizon you're expecting to fine-tune the analysis.

◆

Context

The portfolio consists of 10 early-to-growth-stage start-ups across various industries, with two underperforming in terms of revenue and market share. The investor is weighing the decision to divest or continue supporting these start-ups, considering resource allocation and the potential for a turnaround, given current market dynamics and founder commitment.

Prompt 2: Portfolio management

I manage a portfolio of 10 start-ups, but two are underperforming. How should I decide whether to exit or continue supporting them?

Sample output

1. **Review their KPIs:** Analyse their KPIs over the last 12 months.
2. **Evaluate market conditions:** Determine if external factors, such as market shifts and regulations, are affecting performance.
3. **Assess the founder's vision:** Have a conversation with the founders to understand their plans for a turnaround.
4. **Consider the cost of support:** Calculate the opportunity cost of continuing support versus reallocating resources to stronger start-ups.
5. **Establish a timeline:** Set specific milestones for improvement and a time frame for reassessment.

Tips for customizing

- Specify the types of start-ups in your portfolio (e.g., SaaS, biotech) for more focused exit strategies.
- Include your level of involvement in their operations to tailor the recommendations further.

Role 4: Innovation Strategist

An Innovation Strategist is responsible for identifying new opportunities for growth and driving innovation within an organization. They manage R&D initiatives, explore new markets and implement creative solutions.

◆

Context

The start-up is a logistics company that has prioritized operational efficiency to scale rapidly. However, the leadership recognizes the need to balance efficiency with innovation to maintain long-term competitiveness. The company seeks to shift its culture to encourage creativity and experimentation while still meeting operational goals.

Prompt 1: Fostering innovation culture

How can I create a culture of innovation within a start-up that currently focuses heavily on operational efficiency?

Sample output

1. **Encourage risk-taking:** Create an environment where employees feel safe to experiment and fail without consequences.
2. **Allocate resources for innovation:** Dedicate time and budget for employees to work on new ideas and side projects.
3. **Reward creativity:** Recognize and reward employees who come up with innovative solutions that impact the business.
4. **Build cross-functional teams:** Promote collaboration between different departments to foster diverse thinking.

Tips for customizing

- Specify the type of start-up (e.g., tech, manufacturing) to get tailored advice on fostering innovation.
- Define whether the goal is product innovation or process improvement for more targeted suggestions.

Bonus prompts for start-ups

Pitch deck

You are an expert consultant for start-ups. Assist me in creating an engaging pitch deck for [your start-up's details here], highlighting our unique value proposition, market opportunity and financial projections. Craft a compelling story that attracts investors and secures funding!

Customer persona development

Assume a role of 15 years of hands-on business knowledge. Develop detailed customer personas for [your product/service details here], including demographics, pain points and buying behaviours.

Growth hacking strategies

You are a growth hack expert. Suggest innovative growth hacking strategies to rapidly scale user acquisition for [your start-up details here]. Implement cutting-edge tactics to accelerate your growth exponentially. Understand your audience deeply to tailor your marketing and product development.

Product road map planning

You are an expert product manager. Please outline a 12-month product road map for [your product details], including key features, milestones and timelines. Plan your development to stay on track and meet your goals efficiently!

Perform a competitive analysis for [your business], comparing our strengths, weaknesses, opportunities and threats against those of our top competitors. Stay ahead by knowing where you stand in the market and how to differentiate!

7

Technology, Development and IT Prompts

Technology roles are focused on building, maintaining and scaling digital systems and infrastructure. These roles require problem-solving skills, technical expertise and the ability to adapt to fast-changing technologies and methodologies.

∞

Role 1: Software Developer

A Software Developer designs, codes and maintains software systems. They must ensure that software is scalable, secure and user-friendly.

◆

Context

The web application is built using Node.js back-end with a PostgreSQL database. The issue arises when concurrent users exceed 500, causing response times to increase by 30 per cent. The application has logging enabled but there is no comprehensive performance monitoring system in place.

Prompt 1: Debugging a performance issue

I'm facing a performance issue in a web application. Assume the issue occurs during peak load, and the database query execution is slower than expected. What steps should I take to identify and resolve the issue?

Sample output

1. **Analyse slow queries:** Use PostgreSQL's EXPLAIN command to identify which queries are slow under peak load.
2. **Optimize database indexes:** Ensure that the queries are using proper indexes to speed up search operations.
3. **Check connection pooling:** Review how connections are managed during peak load and optimize the connection pool size for Node.js.
4. **Add caching:** Implement caching at the application layer to reduce the load on the database.
5. **Implement monitoring tools:** Use tools like New Relic or Datadog to monitor application performance in real time.

Tips for customizing

-   Specify whether you're using a cloud service (Amazon Web Service [AWS], Google Cloud Platform [GCP]) to refine server recommendations.
-   Include details on database sharding or partitioning, if applicable.

◆

Context

The feature requires role-based access control (RBAC) for three user roles: Admin, Manager and User. The application currently handles user authentication through OAuth 2.0, but role management has not been set up yet. User data is stored in a PostgreSQL database.

Prompt 2: Implementing a new feature

I need to implement a new feature in our SaaS product for managing user permissions. Assume that the application is built using the React framework on the front-end and a Python/Django back-end. What steps should I follow to ensure secure and efficient implementation?

Sample output

1. **Define role hierarchy:** Outline the permissions for each role (Admin, Manager, User) and map them to the actions they can perform in the application.
2. **Modify back-end:** Implement role-based middleware in Django that checks user roles before executing actions. Leverage Django's User and Group models.
3. **Secure endpoints:** Ensure that the Representational State Transfer Application Programming Interface (REST API) endpoints are protected based on user roles by adding role checks in the view layer.
4. **Front-end implementation:** Create a dynamic interface in React that adjusts available actions based on the user's role.
5. **Test thoroughly:** Write unit and integration tests for both back-end and front-end to ensure role enforcement is consistent across all areas of the application.

Tips for customizing

- Specify if you want to integrate additional features like 2FA or session management.
- Include any performance considerations to fine-tune the solution.

Role 2: AI/ML Engineer

An AI/ML Engineer designs and develops machine learning models and algorithms. They apply AI techniques to solve complex problems while ensuring model performance and accuracy.

◆

Context

You're working with a Python environment using TensorFlow and Keras for model development. The dataset is moderately imbalanced, with 60 per cent of images in one class and 40 per cent in another. The graphics processing unit (GPU) resources are limited, and the goal is to achieve over 90 per cent accuracy.

Prompt 1: Training a new model

I need to train a machine learning model for image classification. Assume that I have a dataset of 10,000 labelled images. What are the steps I should follow to ensure the model is accurate and efficient?

Sample output

1. **Pre-process the dataset:** Normalize the images and apply data augmentation to address the class imbalance.
2. **Choose the right model architecture:** Use a pre-trained model, such as the residual neural network (ResNet) or visual geometry group (VGG), with transfer learning to optimize resource usage.
3. **Tune hyperparameters:** Use techniques like grid search or random search to find the best hyperparameters (learning rate, batch size).
4. **Monitor training:** Implement early stopping and learning rate schedulers to avoid overfitting.

5. **Validate and test:** Set aside a validation set and use it to track model performance during training.

Tips for customizing

- Specify if the model needs to be optimized for edge devices or mobile to get more relevant recommendations.
- Include the nature of the images (e.g., medical, satellite) for domain-specific advice.

◆

Context

The model is trained using PyTorch, and the application is hosted on AWS. You expect real-time text input from thousands of users simultaneously. The system should handle peak loads with minimal latency (under 100ms).

Prompt 2: Deploying an ML model

I've trained a machine learning model for sentiment analysis. How should I deploy this model to handle real-time text data from social media, ensuring scalability and low latency?

Sample output

1. **Containerize the model:** Use Docker to containerize the model and ensure consistent deployment across environments.
2. **Use a model-serving platform:** Deploy the model using AWS SageMaker or TensorFlow Serving for efficient inference.
3. **Set up autoscaling:** Implement autoscaling on AWS to handle peak loads, ensuring the system scales based on demand.
4. **Optimize the model:** Use techniques like quantization or ONNX for faster inference and lower memory consumption.

5. **Monitor performance:** Use real-time monitoring tools like AWS CloudWatch to track system latency and throughput.

Tips for customizing

- Include details about any specific tools or frameworks you want to integrate (e.g., Kubernetes).
- Define your cost limitations for more budget-friendly recommendations.

Role 3: DevOps Engineer

A DevOps Engineer ensures that software development and IT operations teams work together efficiently. They automate processes, manage infrastructure and monitor system performance.

◆

Context

The microservices are written in Go and deployed on Google Kubernetes Engine (GKE). The goal is to minimize deployment downtime and automate testing at each stage.

Prompt 1: Setting up CI/CD pipeline

I'm setting up a CI/CD pipeline[5] for a microservices-based application. Assume that the application uses Docker and Kubernetes. What are the steps to ensure efficient and secure deployment?

---

[5]Continuous integration and continuous delivery (CI/CD) pipeline

1. **Version control:** Use Git for version control, with branches set up for development, staging and production.
2. **Containerization:** Ensure all microservices are Dockerized and stored in a secure Docker registry like Google Container Registry.
3. **Automated testing:** Set up unit, integration and end-to-end tests to run automatically on every code commit.
4. **Deploy with Kubernetes:** Use Kubernetes' RollingUpdate strategy to ensure zero downtime during deployments.
5. **Monitoring and logging:** Implement tools like Prometheus for monitoring and ELK Stack for centralized logging.

Tips for customizing

- Specify if you're using any specific CI/CD tools (e.g., Jenkins, CircleCI) to get tailored integration advice.
- Include security concerns like access control and encryption for more secure pipeline suggestions.

◆

Context

The project requires multiple Elastic Compute Cloud (EC2) instances, load balancers and a relational database service (RDS) instance. The infrastructure should automatically scale based on traffic, and the total budget for the cloud infrastructure is $5,000 per month.

Prompt 2: Automating infrastructure provisioning

I need to automate the provisioning of cloud infrastructure for a new project. Assume the project will run on AWS. What steps should I follow to ensure scalability and cost-efficiency?

1. **Use Infrastructure as Code (IaC):** Implement Terraform or AWS CloudFormation to automate the provisioning process.
2. **Optimize instance types:** Choose the right EC2 instance types (e.g., t3.medium for general workloads) to balance performance and cost.
3. **Set up autoscaling:** Configure autoscaling groups to dynamically adjust the number of EC2 instances based on traffic.
4. **Implement spot instances:** Use spot instances, where applicable, to reduce costs for non-critical workloads.
5. **Monitor costs:** Use AWS Cost Explorer and set up budget alerts to ensure that the infrastructure remains within the $5,000 per month budget.

Tips for customizing

- Specify whether the workload is CPU- or memory-intensive for more precise EC2 recommendations.
- Include any compliance needs (e.g., Health Insurance Portability and Accountability Act [HIPAA], General Data Protection Regulation [GDPR]) for secure infrastructure set-up.

Role 4: IT Manager

An IT Manager oversees the technology infrastructure of a company. They ensure that systems are reliable, secure and optimized for efficiency while managing the IT team.

◆

The company operates in a highly regulated industry (e.g., finance, healthcare) with strict compliance requirements. The current network set-up includes on-premises servers for sensitive data and AWS for scalability.

Prompt 1: Improving network security

I want to improve the network security of our company. Assume that we're using a hybrid cloud infrastructure with on-premises servers and AWS cloud services. What steps should I take to enhance security?

Sample output

1. **Conduct a security audit:** Start by auditing both on-premises and cloud infrastructure to identify potential vulnerabilities.
2. **Implement a Zero Trust model:** Apply Zero Trust principles to enforce strict identity verification for every user or device accessing the network.
3. **Secure data transmission:** Use virtual private networks (VPNs) and encryption (e.g., secure sockets layer [SSL], transport layer security [TLS]) for secure communication between on-premises servers and the cloud.
4. **Monitor network traffic:** Use tools like AWS GuardDuty for monitoring cloud traffic and security information and event management (SIEM) tools for on-premises network monitoring.
5. **Update compliance protocols:** Ensure that the setup adheres to industry-specific regulations like GDPR or HIPAA.

Tips for customizing

- Specify any particular compliance standards to get more tailored advice.

- Include details about the size of the IT team or available budget for security improvements.

◆

Context

The company has grown rapidly, leading to inefficiencies in resource management. The IT team has limited staff, and there is a $100,000 annual budget for IT operations optimization.

Prompt 2: Optimizing IT operations

I need to optimize our IT operations for better efficiency and cost control. Assume we manage a mix of on-premises data centres and cloud infrastructure (AWS and Azure). What steps should I take?

Sample output

1. **Consolidate cloud services:** Evaluate the usage of both AWS and Azure, and consider moving to a single provider, if possible, to reduce costs.
2. **Automate routine tasks:** Implement automation tools like Ansible or Puppet to automate repetitive tasks like system updates and backups.
3. **Monitor resource utilization:** Use cloud monitoring tools (e.g., AWS CloudWatch, Azure Monitor) to track and optimize resource usage in real time.
4. **Streamline helpdesk processes:** Use information technology service management (ITSM) tools like ServiceNow to improve incident management and response times.
5. **Train the team:** Invest in upskilling your IT team to handle new technologies more efficiently.

Tips for customizing

- Specify whether you want to focus more on cost-saving measures or process automation for more targeted recommendations.
- Include any specific tools or vendors that your company uses for IT management.

Role 5: Cybersecurity Specialist

A Cybersecurity Specialist focuses on protecting an organization's IT systems and data from cyberattacks. They develop security strategies, monitor for threats and ensure compliance with regulations.

◆

Context

Breach was detected on an e-commerce platform running on AWS. The compromised data includes customer payment information, and the company must comply with Payment Card Industry Data Security Standard (PCI DSS).

Prompt 1: Responding to a data breach

I've identified a potential data breach in our system. Assume sensitive customer data may have been compromised. What steps should I take to respond and mitigate the damage?

Sample output

1. **Isolate affected systems:** Immediately isolate the compromised servers to prevent further data leakage.
2. **Notify stakeholders:** Inform legal, compliance and senior management about the breach. Notify affected customers, if required by law.

3. **Conduct a forensic investigation:** Engage cybersecurity experts to identify how the breach occurred, which data was compromised, and if the attackers are still inside the system.
4. **Patch vulnerabilities:** Apply patches to all identified vulnerabilities, especially in web applications and servers.
5. **Report and document:** Prepare a detailed incident report, ensuring compliance with PCI DSS requirements, and follow up with a plan to prevent future breaches.

Tips for customizing

- Specify the industry (e.g., e-commerce, healthcare) to get industry-specific compliance and legal steps.
- Include details on whether internal or external cybersecurity teams are involved for tailored advice.

◆

Context

The company is expanding into the European market, making GDPR compliance essential. The current cybersecurity measures are minimal, and the team needs a detailed road map for implementation.

Prompt 2: Building a cybersecurity strategy

I'm tasked with building a comprehensive cybersecurity strategy for our organization. Assume we handle sensitive customer data and must comply with GDPR. What are the key components I should include?

Sample output

1. **Risk assessment:** Start by conducting a thorough risk assessment to identify vulnerabilities in your systems, particularly around data storage and processing.

2. **Data encryption:** Ensure all sensitive customer data, both at rest and in transit, is encrypted using industry-standard protocols like AES-256.
3. **Access controls:** Implement strict access control policies based on least privilege, ensuring only authorized personnel can access sensitive data.
4. **Incident response plan:** Develop and document a clear incident response plan for potential data breaches, ensuring compliance with GDPR's 72-hour reporting requirement.
5. **Employee training:** Conduct regular cybersecurity awareness programmes for employees to reduce risks like phishing attacks.

Tips for customizing

- Define the type of sensitive data (e.g., personal, financial) for more tailored security measures.
- Include budget or resource limitations for more practical advice.

Role 6: UX/UI Designer

A UX/UI Designer focuses on creating user-friendly interfaces that enhance the user experience. They work closely with developers to design intuitive, visually appealing software.

◆

Context

A mobile app with features like workout tracking, nutrition guides and a social component for sharing progress is being built for both iOS and Android, with the goal of maintaining a seamless user experience across devices.

Prompt 1: Designing a mobile app

I'm designing a mobile app for a fitness start-up. Assume that the app needs to appeal to a wide user base, including beginners and fitness experts. What design principles should I follow?

Sample output

1. **Simplify the onboarding process:** Design a user-friendly onboarding flow that requires minimal input and guides users through the app's features.
2. **Create flexible navigation:** Ensure that navigation is intuitive, with clear paths for different user groups (e.g., beginners versus experts).
3. **Use a clean, responsive design:** Opt for a minimalistic design with easy-to-read fonts and responsive elements that work on various screen sizes.
4. **Focus on accessibility:** Ensure the app is accessible to all users, including those with visual or motor impairments, by incorporating features like voice commands and adjustable text sizes.
5. **Implement social features carefully:** Design social sharing features that feel natural and encourage engagement without overwhelming users.

Tips for customizing

- Specify any branding guidelines or colour schemes to get tailored design suggestions.
- Include details on specific features (e.g., workout logging, meal planning) to refine the user interface of the app.

◆

Context

A website built on Shopify serves a global customer base. Recent analytics show that users are abandoning their carts, and the average session time has decreased by 20 per cent in the last three months.

Prompt 2: Improving user engagement

The engagement on our e-commerce website has dropped. Assume that I want to improve the UX/UI to increase conversion rates. What steps should I take?

Sample output

1. **Analyse user behaviour:** Use tools like Google Analytics and Hotjar to identify where users are dropping off during their sessions.
2. **Optimize the checkout process:** Simplify the checkout flow by reducing the number of steps and adding auto-fill options for returning customers.
3. **Improve product descriptions:** Enhance product pages with more detailed descriptions, high-quality images and customer reviews.
4. **Test new layouts:** Run A/B tests on different UI elements (e.g., button placement, colour schemes) to see which versions improve conversion rates.
5. **Enhance mobile experience:** Ensure that the mobile version of the site is fully optimized for speed and ease of use, as many users shop on mobile devices.

Tips for customizing

- Specify if you want to focus on mobile or desktop experiences for more targeted advice.
- Include details about your product categories or target audience for more specific engagement strategies.

Role 7: Mobile App Developer

A Mobile App Developer builds applications for mobile devices, ensuring they are efficient, user-friendly and scalable. They often work with frameworks like React Native or native platforms like Swift (iOS) and Kotlin (Android).

◆

Context

An app has features like real-time notifications, location tracking and a social feed. Users are reporting slow response times and occasional crashes on both iOS and Android devices.

Prompt 1: Optimizing mobile app performance

I'm experiencing performance issues in a mobile app built with React Native. What steps should I take to optimize the app's speed and responsiveness?

Sample output

1. **Reduce bundle size:** Use tools like Webpack to minimize the size of your app's JavaScript bundle.
2. **Optimize images and assets:** Compress images and other static assets to reduce load times, particularly on slower networks.
3. **Minimize unnecessary re-renders:** Review your components to ensure that unnecessary re-renders aren't affecting performance. Use tools like React.memo where applicable.
4. **Profile the app:** Use React Native's performance profiling tools to identify bottlenecks and address memory leaks or slow API calls.
5. **Handle crashes:** Implement crash reporting tools like Sentry to monitor and fix crashes in real time.

Tips for customizing

- Include details about the app's architecture (e.g., state management using Redux) for more targeted advice.
- Specify if you're looking for platform-specific optimizations for iOS or Android.

Special use case: Modify code efficiently

To ensure your AI tool modifies code accurately and comprehensively while adhering to the instruction set and standard practices, you can follow these best practices in your prompts:

1. **Provide clear and detailed instructions**

   - **Be specific:** Clearly specify what needs to be modified and why. For example:
     » Add error handling to the file upload function using try-except.
     » Optimize the code for readability by adding comments and renaming variables for clarity.
   - **Highlight areas of change:** If the modification applies to only part of the code, mention the exact sections or lines.
   - **Mention non-negotiable requirements:** State any elements that must not be removed or altered.

2. **Share complete code**

   - **Provide context:** Always share the entire code or a representative portion of it. Without context, modifications may miss dependencies or relationships.
   - If your code has thousands of lines, you should provide function/class with more text for better results.
   - **Include imports and dependencies:** Include library imports, configurations and initialization steps.

3. **Describe expected behaviour**

- **Functional expectations:** Explain what the modified code should accomplish.
- **Error and edge case handling:** Define how the code should handle errors, exceptions or specific edge cases.
- **Example:** Ensure the code retries the operation three times in case of failure before exiting gracefully with a log message.

4. **Request adherence to standards**

- **Mention best practices:** Specify standards or practices to follow, such as:
    » PEP 8, or Python Enhancement Proposal 8, for Python
    » OWASP, or the Open Worldwide Application Security Project, for security
    » SOLID principles[6] for object-oriented programming
- **Avoid ambiguity:** For example, instead of saying 'Make it secure', say, 'Use prepared statements to prevent SQL injection'.

5. **Validate the output**

- **Ask for explanations:** Request a breakdown of the changes made to ensure that the modifications align with your expectations.
- **Run test cases:** Provide test cases or scenarios to validate the correctness of the modified code.
- **Request comments in code:** Ask for inline comments to understand logic changes.

---

[6]The SOLID principles are a set of five design principles: Single Responsibility Principle (SRP), Open-Closed Principle (OCP), Liskov Substitution Principle (LSP), Interface Segregation Principle (ISP) and Dependency Inversion Principle (DIP).

6. Ask for incremental changes

- **Iterative approach:** Request changes step by step rather than in one go to ensure no part of the instruction is missed.
- **Example:** First, add logging to the functions. Once that's done, implement retry logic for the API calls.

7. Encourage holistic thinking

- **Context beyond the code:** If the task involves implementing a feature based on industry standards, explicitly mention it.
  - » **Example:** Ensure this API follows RESTful principles.
- **Ask for alternatives:** Request suggestions for better practices.
  - » **Example:** Is there a more efficient algorithm for this function?

8. Ask for assurance on completeness

- **Use prompts such as:**
  - » Ensure all components of the existing code are retained and no functionality is lost while implementing these changes.
  - » Review the changes against industry standards and ensure no best practices are violated.

9. Specify the environment

- Mention the programming language version, libraries or the runtime environment the code is intended for.
  - » **Example:** This Python code runs on version 3.10 with the Requests library.

10. Verify outputs with examples

- Provide sample inputs and expected outputs. Request the modified code to be tested against these.

- **Example:** Given input X, the output should be Y. Ensure the code achieves this.

Checklist for care

1. **Review generated output:** Always double-check the output for accuracy.
2. **Test rigorously:** Run the modified code in your environment to verify correctness.
3. **Iterate if necessary:** If something is missed, refine your instructions and request updates.
4. **Combine human expertise:** Use ChatGPT for enhancements but validate using personal or team expertise to ensure completeness and adherence to domain-specific nuances.

By following these steps, you can make ChatGPT a reliable assistant for modifying code without missing essential components or violating standard practices.

8

Sales, Marketing and Communications Prompts

Role 1: Sales Executive

A Sales Executive is responsible for generating leads, closing deals and building strong customer relationships. They play a critical role in driving revenue growth and meeting sales targets through effective communication, negotiation and presentation skills.

◆

Context

A SaaS product automates and enhances customer support functions. Your target market consists of companies with 100–500 employees in the US healthcare industry. You are currently using customer relationship management (CRM) software like HubSpot and have a sales team of five people.

Prompt 1: Building a sales pipeline

I need to build a sales pipeline for a new B2B SaaS product that streamlines customer service operations. Assume that I'm targeting mid-sized companies in the healthcare industry. What steps should I follow?

1. **Research your target market:** Understand the unique needs of healthcare companies, focusing on compliance and customer service automation.
2. **Segment your leads:** Use your CRM to create specific lead segments based on company size, location and needs.
3. **Generate qualified leads:** Focus on content marketing (e.g., whitepapers, webinars) to attract healthcare companies looking to improve customer service.
4. **Nurture leads:** Set up automated email campaigns to nurture leads with relevant content before moving to the next stage.
5. **Close deals:** Use a consultative approach to demonstrate the SaaS product's value in improving the company's customer service efficiency and compliance with healthcare regulations.

Tips for customizing

- Specify whether your sales process is inbound or outbound to receive more tailored advice.
- Include details about your CRM and lead management tools to get more focused strategies.

◆

Context

A product is priced 15 per cent higher than that of competitors but offers advanced automation features and 24/7 customer support. The prospect is a growing healthcare company that values long-term scalability and reliability.

Prompt 2: Overcoming price objections

A potential customer is concerned that our product's price is too high compared to that of competitors. Assume our product includes more features and better customer support. How should I address their concern?

Sample output

1. **Acknowledge the concern:** Empathize with the customer and agree that pricing is an important consideration.
2. **Reframe the value:** Highlight how your product's additional features (e.g., advanced automation and 24/7 support) will save them money and improve efficiency in the long run.
3. **Show ROI:** Provide case studies or metrics showing how similar healthcare companies have reduced costs and improved customer satisfaction using your product.
4. **Offer flexibility:** Suggest flexible payment plans or scalable options that align with their budget without compromising key features.
5. **Close confidently:** Reassure them that investing in a higher-quality solution now will prevent costly inefficiencies down the road.

Tips for customizing

- Include details about competitors' pricing and features for more specific comparisons.
- State clearly whether the customer is more concerned with short-term or long-term value to adjust the conversation.

◆

Context

You're targeting mid-sized healthcare companies and have been generating a steady stream of leads through inbound marketing (e.g., blog content, webinars). However, the current conversion rate from lead to customer is only 5 per cent, and you want to raise it to at least 10 per cent.

Prompt 3: Increasing conversion rates

I want to improve the conversion rate of our leads to paying customers. Assume we're using an inbound sales strategy and HubSpot CRM. What steps can I take to increase conversions?

Sample output

1. **Qualify leads more effectively:** Use lead scoring in HubSpot to prioritize leads that are more likely to convert based on their engagement and company size.
2. **Optimize follow-up process:** Set up automated follow-up emails and notifications for sales reps to ensure timely and personalized outreach.
3. **Tailor the sales pitch:** Use data from previous conversations to craft personalized sales pitches that focus on the prospect's pain points.
4. **Offer limited-time incentives:** Provide incentives, such as discounted onboarding or extended trials, to create urgency and encourage quicker decisions.
5. **Analyse and iterate:** Regularly review your conversion data and adjust strategies based on what's working. For example, if leads respond well to specific content, adjust your follow-up messages accordingly.

Tips for customizing

- Specify the type of content your inbound strategy uses (e.g., blog posts, webinars) to refine conversion advice.
- Include details about your average sales cycle for more focused recommendations on timing and follow-up strategies.

Role 2: Marketing Professional

A Marketing Professional develops and executes strategies

to promote a company's products or services. They focus on increasing brand awareness, generating leads and driving conversions through various channels.

◆

Context

A clothing brand uses organic materials, has ethical manufacturing processes and offers a subscription-based service for sustainable clothing. The company is looking to drive online sales through Instagram, Facebook and Google Ads.

Prompt 1: Creating a digital marketing campaign

I need to create a digital marketing campaign for a new eco-friendly clothing brand. Assume that the target audience is millennials in the US who value sustainability. What should the campaign focus on?

Sample output

1. **Emphasize sustainability:** Focus the messaging on how eco-conscious millennials can reduce their environmental footprint by choosing organic and ethically made clothing.
2. **Use storytelling:** Create video content that tells the brand's story, showcasing the manufacturing process and commitment to sustainability.
3. **Leverage influencers:** Partner with eco-conscious influencers who resonate with your target demographic to amplify your message.
4. **Incorporate discounts:** Offer limited-time discounts or promotions for new subscribers to drive conversions.
5. **Track and optimize:** Use Google Analytics and Facebook Pixel to monitor campaign performance and adjust targeting based on engagement and sales.

Tips for customizing

- Include additional marketing channels like email or TikTok for broader reach.
- Specify whether you want to focus more on brand awareness or direct sales to tailor the strategy.

◆

Context

A marketing email was sent to 5,000 subscribers, promoting a new feature in your SaaS product. The open rate was 10 per cent, and the click-through rate (CTR) was 2 per cent, significantly lower than previous campaigns.

Prompt 2: Analysing campaign performance

Our latest email marketing campaign had a low open rate and CTR. Assume that the target audience consists of existing customers in the B2B space. How can I analyse what went wrong?

Sample output

1. **Evaluate subject lines:** Analyse whether the subject lines were engaging enough to encourage higher open rates. Consider A/B testing different headlines.
2. **Check segmentation:** Ensure that the email list was properly segmented. If the promotion wasn't relevant to certain customers, it may have led to lower engagement.
3. **Examine email content:** Review the email's body content, design and call to action (CTA). Was the messaging clear? Were there too many distractions?
4. **Timing and frequency:** Consider whether the email was sent at the wrong time or too frequently, which may have contributed to fatigue among subscribers.
5. **Review past performance:** Compare this campaign with

previous ones to identify any significant differences in design, messaging or audience.

Tips for customizing

- Include details about the type of SaaS product to get more relevant content analysis.
- Specify whether you want to optimize for different metrics (e.g., conversion rate) to tailor the recommendations.

Role 3: Real Estate Agent

A Real Estate Agent helps clients buy, sell or rent properties. They need to be adept at understanding the market, negotiating deals and marketing properties effectively.

◆

Context

The property is a luxury home located in an exclusive neighbourhood with high demand. The selling points include a custom-built design, expansive outdoor spaces and proximity to premium amenities (e.g., golf courses, private schools).

Prompt 1: Marketing a high-end property

I need to create a marketing strategy to sell a high-end residential property in a competitive market. Assume that the target buyers are affluent individuals. What should the strategy focus on?

Sample output

1. **Highlight unique features:** Focus on the custom-built design, luxury finishes and unique amenities that set the property apart from others.

2. **Use professional photography and videography:** Invest in high-quality visuals, including drone footage, to showcase the property's features.

3. **Leverage virtual tours:** Offer virtual tours or 3D walkthroughs to attract out-of-town buyers who may not be able to visit in person.

4. **Target affluent buyers:** Run targeted ads on platforms like Instagram and LinkedIn aimed at high-net-worth individuals. Utilize real estate portals like MagicBricks and Makaan.com. (You can replace these portal names with your preferred portals.)

5. **Host exclusive open houses:** Organize private, invite-only events for prospective buyers, offering an upscale experience during the viewing.

Tips for customizing

- Include any details about specific buyer preferences (e.g., family-focused, tech-savvy) for more personalized strategies.
- Specify whether you're focusing on local or international buyers for better ad targeting.

◆

Context

A property is located in a mid-range neighbourhood with homes selling for an average of ₹5,00,00,000. The client has listed the property for ₹6,00,00,000 believing its unique features justify the higher price.

Prompt 2: Handling client expectations

A client wants to sell their property at a price that's above market value. Assume that the property has been on the market for three months with minimal interest. How should I approach this situation?

1. **Present market data:** Share recent comparable sales data to show the client the current market trends and the gap between their asking price and market value.
2. **Highlight the risks:** Explain the risks of overpricing, such as longer time on the market and potential buyers viewing the property as undesirable.
3. **Suggest a pricing strategy:** Recommend a gradual price reduction strategy over the next few weeks to generate more interest.
4. **Enhance marketing efforts:** Offer to invest in additional marketing strategies, such as video tours or staging, to increase visibility.
5. **Keep communication open:** Maintain a positive and empathetic tone to ensure the client feels heard and understood throughout the process.

Tips for customizing

- Include details about the client's priorities (e.g., quick sale, maximizing profit) to offer more targeted solutions.
- Specify any unique features of the property to refine the conversation around value.

Role 4: Travel Agent

A Travel Agent helps clients plan and book travel experiences, whether for business or leisure. They offer personalized recommendations and ensure smooth arrangements for transportation, accommodation and activities.

Context

A family is interested in a mix of cultural experiences, outdoor activities and kid-friendly attractions. They want to visit major cities like Tokyo, Kyoto and Osaka.

Prompt 1: Creating a custom travel itinerary

I need to create a 10-day travel itinerary for a family vacation to Japan. Assume that the family has two children, ages 8 and 12. What should the itinerary include?

Sample output

1. **Days 1–2 (Tokyo):** Visit cultural sites like the Senso-ji temple and Meiji shrine. Include a fun visit to Tokyo Disneyland for the kids.
2. **Days 3–4 (Mount Fuji):** Plan a day trip to Mount Fuji for scenic views and light hiking. Offer a relaxing stay at a ryokan (traditional inn) with hot springs.
3. **Days 5–7 (Kyoto):** Explore the historical sites of Kyoto, including Kinkaku-ji (Golden Pavilion) and the Fushimi Inari shrine. Offer a kid-friendly activity like a traditional Japanese tea ceremony.
4. **Days 8–9 (Osaka):** Include a visit to the Osaka Castle and Universal Studios Japan for fun family entertainment.
5. **Day 10 (Departure):** Schedule free time for shopping and final sightseeing before departure.

Tips for customizing

- Include preferences for accommodation types (e.g., hotels, vacation rentals) to get tailored recommendations.
- Specify any dietary restrictions or activity preferences for more personalized itineraries.

◆

Context

The client has an important business meeting scheduled for the next day in Paris and needs to arrive on time. They have a flexible budget but want the quickest and most reliable option.

Prompt 2: Handling last-minute travel changes

A client's international flight was cancelled, and they need to make alternative travel arrangements within the next 24 hours. Assume the client is travelling from New York to Paris for business. What should I do?

Sample output

1. **Find alternative flights:** Search for alternative flights departing from nearby airports (e.g., Newark or Philadelphia) and prioritize direct flights to reduce the risk of further delays.
2. **Book a backup flight:** If available, book two options—one from the current airport and one from a nearby airport—to ensure the client has flexibility.
3. **Arrange quick transport:** Offer a car service to transport the client to a different airport if needed.
4. **Notify the hotel and business contacts:** Inform the client's hotel in Paris of the delay and ensure early check-in availability. Notify business contacts of any changes to the meeting time.
5. **Offer in-transit solutions:** If the client needs to work during travel, offer inflight Wi-Fi and arrange airport lounge access for comfort.

Tips for customizing

- Include details about the client's frequent flyer status or preferred airlines for better booking options.
- Specify any meeting rescheduling constraints to prioritize faster or alternative transportation solutions.

∾

Role 5: Advertising Manager

An Advertising Manager oversees the creation, planning and execution of ad campaigns. They focus on increasing brand awareness, driving traffic and generating sales through paid media channels.

◆

Context

The target audience consists of millennials and Gen Z users in the US who are interested in budgeting and managing student loans. You're planning to run ads on Instagram, TikTok and YouTube.

Prompt 1: Developing a social media ad campaign

I need to develop a social media ad campaign for a new mobile app. Assume that the app helps users manage their personal finances. What should the campaign focus on?

Sample output

1. **Focus on pain points:** Highlight common financial challenges faced by your target audience, such as managing student loans, creating a budget and saving for future goals.
2. **Demonstrate the solution:** Show how the app simplifies budgeting, tracks expenses and provides personalized financial tips.
3. **Use video and influencers:** Leverage short-form video content on TikTok and Instagram to demonstrate how the app works, and partner with influencers to amplify the message.
4. **Incorporate testimonials:** Share testimonials or success stories from early users who have achieved financial success using the app.
5. **Offer a promotion:** Provide a limited-time discount or

incentive (e.g., free trial or premium feature) to encourage sign-ups.

Tips for customizing

- Include details about the app's key features (e.g., real-time alerts, investment tracking) to tailor the messaging.
- Specify whether you want to focus on direct conversions or brand awareness for better ad targeting.

◆

Context

A campaign is promoting eco-friendly home products (e.g., reusable kitchen items) and has a CTR of 5 per cent but a conversion rate of only 1 per cent. The store's landing page is optimized for search engine optimization (SEO) and mobile responsiveness.

Prompt 2: Analysing ad performance

The latest Google Ads campaign for our online store has a high CTR but low conversion rate. Assume that the ads are targeting people interested in eco-friendly products. How should I analyse the campaign and improve it?

Sample output

1. **Review the landing page:** Ensure that the landing page is aligned with the ad messaging and includes a clear CTA. Check for any elements that may confuse or distract visitors.
2. **Evaluate targeting:** Double-check the targeting settings in Google Ads to ensure that the ads are reaching the right audience. Narrow the targeting if necessary to focus on more qualified leads.
3. **Test ad copy and design:** Run A/B tests on different ad variations, including headlines, descriptions and

visuals, to identify which combinations lead to higher conversions.

4. **Analyse pricing or offers:** Review the product pricing or offer (e.g., free shipping, discount) to ensure it's competitive and appealing to eco-conscious consumers.
5. **Check for technical issues:** Ensure that there are no technical issues, such as slow page load times or broken links, that may prevent users from completing the purchase.

Tips for customizing

- Specify the ad budget or duration to get more targeted advice on optimizing the campaign.
- Include details about the sales funnel (e.g., product page, checkout process) to refine the conversion strategy.

9

Legal, Government and Policy Prompts

Role 1: Advocate (Lawyer)

An Advocate (Lawyer) in India provides legal representation, specializing in areas such as property law, corporate law and litigation. They ensure that their client's interests are protected while adhering to Indian laws.

Prompt 1: Drafting a commercial lease agreement

I need to draft a commercial lease agreement. Assume I'm representing the landlord, and the property is a retail space in Mumbai. The lease term is for five years, and I need to ensure that the lease complies with Indian laws, particularly those related to commercial leases, while protecting my client's interests. What clauses should I include? Cover the following points in your response:

1. Rent and payment terms
2. Maintenance and repairs
3. Subleasing restrictions
4. Termination clause
5. Security deposit
6. Dispute resolution
7. Force majeure

Tips for customizing

- Modify based on location-specific laws and tax regulations like Goods and Services Tax (GST).
- Follow-up prompt can provide more details about each clause.

Prompt 2: Preparing legal notice for non-payment of rent

My client, a landlord, has not received rent for three months from a commercial tenant. Assume I need to draft a legal notice demanding payment under Indian laws. What key points should the notice include? Cover the following points in your response.

1. Details of the property and lease agreement
2. Outstanding amount
3. Demand for payment
4. Legal consequences
5. Time frame for compliance
6. Signature and legal authority

Tip for customizing: Tailor the notice based on the lease terms and applicable state tenancy laws.

Role 2: Government Officer

A Government Officer in India is responsible for administering public policies, managing resources, and ensuring compliance with laws and regulations. They play a critical role in governance, public administration and development projects.

Prompt 1: Managing a government infrastructure project

I'm overseeing a government infrastructure project in Rajasthan. Assume that I need to ensure timely completion while adhering to public procurement norms. What steps should I follow to manage this project efficiently? Cover the following points in your response.

1. Review of contracts and tenders
2. Monitoring and reporting
3. Vendor and stakeholder management
4. Environmental and safety compliance
5. Budget and resource allocation

Tips for Customizing

- Adjust based on the type of infrastructure project (e.g., road, water supply).
- Include follow-up steps for managing local community concerns.

Prompt 2: Implementing digital governance in a district

As a district magistrate, I need to implement digital governance in my district to improve public service delivery. Assume that the population is predominantly rural. What initiatives should I prioritize? Cover the following points in your response.

1. Setting up online service portals
2. Digitizing records and documentation
3. Making available e-governance tools for public grievances
4. Raising digital literacy in rural areas
5. Monitoring and transparency tools

Tip for customizing: Recommend specific e-governance platforms or applications based on the district's demographics.

Role 3: Politician

A Politician represents the public, proposes new policies and advocates for laws that align with the interests of their constituents. They engage in legislative, developmental and public welfare work while building consensus among stakeholders.

Prompt 1: Proposing a policy for rural employment

As a member of the Legislative Assembly (MLA) representing a rural constituency in Uttar Pradesh, I need to propose a policy to address unemployment. Assume the budget is limited and there is high demand for jobs. What key initiatives should I include? Cover the following points in your response.

1. Skill development programmes
2. Promotion of micro, small and medium enterprises (MSMEs)
3. Incentives for agri-based industries
4. Public works projects
5. Microfinance and loan schemes

Tip for customizing: Adjust based on the specific industries or natural resources available in the constituency.

Prompt 2: Addressing public health challenges

As an MP representing a large urban area, I need to propose policies to improve public health services. Assume that the area has a shortage of healthcare workers and hospital infrastructure. What policy solutions should I focus on? Cover the following points in your response.

1. Training and incentivizing healthcare workers
2. Public–private partnerships for hospital construction
3. Mobile health clinics
4. Health awareness campaigns
5. Telemedicine solutions

Tip for customizing: Tailor the initiatives based on the health statistics and specific healthcare needs of the constituency.

∞

Role 4: Legal Consultant

A Legal Consultant provides expert legal advice to businesses, government agencies and individuals, focusing on regulatory compliance, contracts and litigation avoidance. They ensure that clients follow legal frameworks while protecting their interests.

Prompt 1: Advising a company on regulatory compliance

I'm advising an Indian tech company expanding into the European market. Assume they must comply with GDPR and other local regulations. What steps should I recommend to ensure full compliance? Cover the following points in your response.

1. Appoint a Data Protection Officer (DPO)
2. Implement data encryption and anonymization
3. Obtain explicit consent for data collection
4. Ensure GDPR compliance of third-party vendors
5. Establish an incident response plan

Tip for customizing: Modify based on the type of data being handled (e.g., healthcare, financial data).

Prompt 2: Reviewing a contract for a foreign client

A foreign client wants to enter into a joint venture with an Indian company. Assume that I'm reviewing the contract. What clauses should I focus on to protect my foreign client's interests under Indian law? Cover the following points in your response.

1. Governing law and jurisdiction
2. Profit sharing and investment terms
3. Dispute resolution mechanism
4. Termination clauses
5. Confidentiality and IP rights

Tip for customizing: Customize the contract review based on industry-specific regulations (e.g., technology, manufacturing).

Role 5: Policy Advisor

A Policy Advisor works closely with government officials, political leaders and organizations to develop, analyse and recommend policy initiatives. They ensure that policy proposals are aligned with public welfare, economic goals and legal frameworks.

Prompt 1: Drafting a policy for affordable housing

I've been tasked with drafting a policy on affordable housing in a growing urban area. Assume that land costs are high and there is a shortage of low-income housing. What elements should I focus on? Cover the following points in your response.

1. Public–private partnerships for construction
2. Subsidies and tax incentives for builders
3. Rent-to-own schemes
4. Alignment with the Pradhan Mantri Awas Yojana (PMAY)
5. Green building practices

Tip for customizing: Customize based on specific city demographics and land availability.

Prompt 2: Recommending a policy to reduce carbon emissions

I'm advising the government on reducing carbon emissions. Assume that the country is industrializing rapidly and faces international pressure to meet environmental targets. What should my policy recommendations include? Cover the following points in your response.

1. Incentives for renewable energy projects
2. Carbon taxation on high emission industries
3. Promotion of electric vehicles
4. Energy efficiency standards for buildings
5. Public awareness campaigns on carbon footprint reduction

Tip for customizing: Adapt based on specific industry requirements and international agreements on emissions targets.

Role 6: Regulatory Affairs Manager

A Regulatory Affairs Manager ensures that the business complies with government regulations, particularly in industries like pharmaceuticals, food and consumer goods. They manage the regulatory approval process, monitor compliance and advise on legislative changes.

Prompt 1: Managing regulatory compliance for a pharma product

I'm working for a pharmaceutical company, and we are launching a new drug in India. Assume that I need to ensure compliance with the Drugs and Cosmetics Act, 1940. What steps should I follow? Cover the following points in your response.

1. Submit clinical trial data to Central Drugs Standard Control Organization (CDSCO)
2. Ensure compliance with labelling regulations
3. Obtain marketing authorization and drug licence
4. Monitor post-marketing safety
5. Ensure good manufacturing practice (GMP) compliance for manufacturing facilities

Tip for customizing: Specify whether the drug is generic or biologic for more specific compliance steps.

10

Finance, Accounting and Risk Management Prompts

Role 1: Financial Analyst

A Financial Analyst is responsible for analysing financial data, creating financial models and providing insights to help companies make informed decisions about investments, budgeting and cost optimization.

Prompt 1: Preparing a financial forecast

I need to prepare a five-year financial forecast for a manufacturing company. Assume that the company plans to expand its operations, and I need to account for potential fluctuations in raw material costs. What key elements should I include in the forecast?

Sample output

1. Revenue projections
2. Cost of goods sold
3. Operating expenses
4. Capital expenditures
5. Cash flow projections

Tips for customizing

- Modify based on industry-specific costs or revenue models.
- Follow-up prompts can focus on sensitivity analysis for raw material cost fluctuations.

Prompt 2: Analysing company's financial health

I'm tasked with analysing the financial health of a retail company. Assume that I need to prepare a report for investors. What financial ratios and metrics should I prioritize?

Sample output

1. Liquidity ratios (e.g., current ratio, quick ratio)
2. Profitability ratios (e.g., net profit margin, return on equity)
3. Efficiency ratios (e.g., inventory turnover, asset turnover)
4. Debt ratios (e.g., debt-to-equity ratio)
5. Market valuation ratios (e.g., price-to-earnings ratio)

Tips for customizing

- Adjust the ratios based on the industry (e.g., debt ratios for capital-intensive sectors).
- Consider adding follow-up prompts for more detailed benchmarking against industry standards.

∞

Role 2: Accountant

An Accountant manages financial records, ensures compliance with tax regulations and provides accurate financial reporting. They play a key role in maintaining a company's financial integrity.

Prompt 1: Preparing year-end financial statements

I need to prepare year-end financial statements for a small business. Assume I'm responsible for ensuring accuracy and compliance with Indian accounting standards. What all should I include?

Sample output

1. Balance sheet
2. Income statement
3. Cash flow statement
4. Statement of changes in equity
5. Notes to financial statements

Tips for customizing

- Modify based on company structure or sector-specific reporting needs.
- Follow-up prompts can dive into detailed requirements of Indian Generally Accepted Accounting Principles (GAAP) or International Financial Reporting Standards (IFRS).

Prompt 2: Managing accounts payable

As the accountant with a mid-sized company, I need to improve the accounts payable process. Assume that I need to streamline payments and reduce processing time. What steps should I take?

Sample output

1. Automate invoice processing
2. Implement early payment discounts
3. Reconcile accounts regularly
4. Establish clear payment terms with vendors
5. Track outstanding payments

Tips for customizing:

- Adjust based on the company's payment cycle or software used for accounting.
- Follow-up prompts can address common challenges in managing vendor relationships.

∞

Role 3: Risk Manager

A Risk Manager identifies, assesses and mitigates financial, operational and strategic risks within a company. They develop risk management frameworks and ensure the organization's stability.

Prompt 1: Developing a risk management framework

I need to develop a risk management framework for a financial services company. Assume the focus is on compliance, operational and market risks. What key components should I include in the framework?

Sample output

1. Risk identification
2. Risk assessment and prioritization
3. Risk mitigation strategies
4. Risk monitoring and reporting
5. Compliance and regulatory adherence

Tips for customizing

- Customize based on the company's specific risk areas (e.g., credit risk, cybersecurity).
- Consider follow-up prompts to dive into tools and metrics for ongoing risk assessment.

Prompt 2: Assessing credit risk in a loan portfolio

I'm responsible for assessing the credit risk of a loan portfolio for a bank. Assume that I need to account for both individual borrower risk and overall portfolio risk. What factors should I analyse?

Sample output

1. Borrower credit scores and history
2. Debt-to-income ratios

3. Loan-to-value ratios
4. Diversification and concentration of portfolio
5. Economic and market conditions

Tips for customizing

- Adjust based on the type of loans (e.g., personal, commercial).
- Follow-up prompts could focus on stress testing and scenario analysis for portfolio stability.

Role 4: Tax Consultant

A Tax Consultant advises clients on tax planning, compliance and filing strategies to minimize tax liability while adhering to legal requirements.

Prompt 1: Advising a client on tax savings for a business

I'm advising a small business client on tax-saving opportunities. Assume that the business operates in India and the client wants to minimize their tax liability legally. What strategies should I recommend?

Sample output

Note: Enable DeepThink or Deep Research in your AI tool for better output)

1. Claiming deductions on business expenses
2. Using depreciation benefits on assets
3. Utilizing tax-saving investments
4. Taking advantage of start-up exemptions
5. Setting up a trust or Hindu Undivided Family (HUF), if applicable

Tips for customizing

- Modify based on the type of business (e.g., service-oriented, manufacturing).
- Include follow-up prompts to explore sector-specific tax deductions.

Prompt 2: Preparing for GST compliance

A client's company recently crossed the GST registration threshold. Assume I need to guide them through the GST registration and compliance process in India. What steps should I follow?

Sample output

1. Register for GST through the government portal
2. Classify goods and services for correct GST rates
3. Set up invoicing and filing systems
4. Maintain proper records of purchases and sales
5. Prepare for monthly, quarterly and annual GST filings

Tips for customizing

- Tailor based on the client's industry and specific GST requirements.
- Follow-up prompts can delve into common GST filing errors and penalties.

Role 5: Internal Auditor

An Internal Auditor evaluates a company's internal controls, risk management and governance processes to ensure compliance and operational efficiency.

Prompt 1: Conducting an internal audit for financial controls

I need to conduct an internal audit of the financial controls in place for a manufacturing company. Assume that the audit must ensure compliance with Indian regulations and identify any weaknesses. What steps should I follow?

Sample output

1. Review financial reporting processes
2. Assess control procedures for cash and bank transactions
3. Verify accounts receivable and payable
4. Evaluate inventory and asset management controls
5. Report findings and recommend corrective actions

Tips for customizing

*   Modify based on industry-specific regulations.
*   Follow-up prompts can focus on tools for tracking compliance issues.

Prompt 2: Auditing for fraud detection

As an internal auditor, I need to conduct an audit focused on fraud detection for a retail company. Assume that I need to assess potential risks in inventory management and cash handling. What areas should I focus on?

Sample output

1. Analyse inventory records for discrepancies
2. Evaluate cash handling and reconciliation procedures
3. Monitor high-value transactions for unusual patterns
4. Assess vendor and supplier relations
5. Review access control and segregation of duties

Tips for customizing

- Adjust based on the company's transaction volume and cash flow.
- Follow-up prompts can suggest fraud detection software or tools.

Role 6: Financial Controller

A Financial Controller oversees financial reporting, budgeting and compliance within an organization. They ensure financial accuracy and support strategic decision-making.

Prompt 1: Preparing an annual budget

I'm responsible for preparing an annual budget for a tech company. Assume that the company is in a growth phase and expects revenue to increase by 30 per cent next year. What sections should I include in the budget?

Sample output

1. Revenue forecast
2. Operating expenses
3. Capital expenditure
4. Cash flow projections
5. Contingency reserves

Tips for customizing

- Modify based on the business model and industry trends.
- Include follow-up prompts for budgeting software recommendations.

Prompt 2: Ensuring compliance with financial regulations

As the Financial Controller, I need to ensure that our company complies with all financial regulations in India. Assume the company is publicly traded. What compliance areas should I prioritize?

Sample output

1. Securities and Exchange Board of India (SEBI) reporting requirements
2. Tax compliance (direct and indirect taxes)
3. Corporate governance and financial disclosure
4. Adherence to auditing standards
5. Internal financial controls and documentation

Tips for customizing

- Adjust based on the industry's regulatory landscape.
- Follow-up prompts could explore recent changes in Indian financial regulations.

11

Education, Research and Mentorship Prompts

Role 1: Teacher

A Teacher is responsible for delivering lessons, assessing student progress and creating a positive learning environment. They play a key role in shaping students' understanding, knowledge and critical thinking skills, while adhering to curriculum guidelines like Central Board of Secondary Education (CBSE) or Indian Certificate of Secondary Education (ICSE).

Prompt 1: Creating a lesson plan

I need to create a lesson plan for a high school history class on the Indian independence movement. Assume the lesson should be interactive and align with the CBSE curriculum. What elements should I include in the lesson plan?

Sample output

1. Learning objectives
2. Engagement activities (e.g., discussions on key leaders, timeline creation)
3. Multimedia tools (videos or images of historical events)
4. Assessment through quizzes or short projects
5. Homework assignment or reflection

Tips for customizing

- Adjust based on the specific chapter or focus within the independence movement.
- Follow-up prompt can provide suggestions for age-appropriate multimedia resources.

Prompt 2: Assessing student progress

I'm responsible for assessing student progress in a middle school English class. Assume I need to evaluate both comprehension and writing skills. What assessment methods should I use?

Sample output

1. Weekly reading comprehension quizzes
2. Essay writing and short-answer tests
3. Project-based assessments on literature themes
4. Class participation and oral recitations
5. Feedback sessions for individual improvement

Tips for customizing

- Modify based on grammar, vocabulary, etc.
- Follow-up prompts could focus on incorporating self-assessment techniques.

Prompt 3: Managing classroom behaviour

I'm teaching a primary school class in an Indian public school, and I need strategies to manage disruptive behaviour effectively. Assume the class includes students from diverse backgrounds and learning needs. What strategies should I implement?

Sample output

1. Establish clear, simple rules with visual aids
2. Use positive reinforcement (reward system)
3. Assign classroom roles for responsibility
4. Encourage group activities to build peer relationships

5. Provide special support for students with learning challenges

Tips for customizing

- Adjust strategies based on specific behavioural challenges observed.
- Follow-up prompts could provide strategies for handling persistent disruptions.

Role 2: Educational Administrator

An Educational Administrator in India manages school operations, enforces educational policies and works to improve the quality of education. They oversee the development of curriculum standards, teacher training and student support services.

Prompt 1: Implementing a school-wide discipline policy

I need to implement a discipline policy in a government school. Assume the school serves students from diverse socio-economic backgrounds. What elements should be included in the policy to ensure fairness and effectiveness?

Sample output

1. Clear guidelines on acceptable behaviour
2. Progressive discipline system (warnings, detentions, etc.)
3. Positive reinforcement and reward programmes
4. Parental involvement for serious cases
5. Periodic policy review for ensuring its relevance

Tips for customizing

- Adjust based on school type and age group.
- Follow-up prompts could include methods to involve community feedback.

Prompt 2: Organizing teacher training programmes

I need to organize a training programme for teachers in a rural area school to improve teaching methods. Assume limited access to technology. What should the training programme focus on?

Sample output

1. Interactive and student-centred teaching techniques
2. Basic classroom management strategies
3. Creative use of limited resources (chalkboard, textbooks)
4. Assessment methods for student progress
5. Incorporating local cultural contexts in lessons

Tips for customizing

- Adjust topics based on the specific educational challenges in the region.
- Follow-up prompts could provide content for individual modules in the training.

Prompt 3: Developing a curriculum for extracurricular activities

I'm tasked with developing a curriculum for extracurricular activities in a CBSE school. Assume that we need to focus on holistic development and cater to both primary and secondary students. What should the curriculum include?

Sample output

1. Physical activities (sports, yoga)
2. Creative arts (dance, drama, music)
3. Social awareness programmes (environmental clubs, community service)
4. Life skills development (public speaking, teamwork)
5. Student councils and leadership roles

Tips for customizing

- Modify based on the age group or cultural interests of students.
- Follow-up prompts could explore individual activity guides for each section.

Role 3: Researcher

A Researcher conducts studies, analyses data and contributes to knowledge in various fields, such as science, social sciences and humanities. They focus on creating impactful research that aligns with local needs and global standards.

Prompt 1: Designing a research proposal

I need to design a research proposal on the impact of online education in rural India. Assume that the study will involve both qualitative and quantitative data collection. What sections should I include in the proposal?

Sample output

1. Introduction and background
2. Research objectives
3. Methodology (sample selection, data collection methods)
4. Expected outcomes and impact
5. Budget and timeline

Tips for customizing

- Tailor based on the specific academic discipline.
- Follow-up prompts could focus on methods for collecting qualitative data in rural areas.

Prompt 2: Conducting a literature review

I am conducting a literature review on mental health trends among youth in India. Assume that I need to find recent studies and credible sources. What steps should I take to complete this review effectively?

Sample output

1. Identify key themes and keywords
2. Search academic journals and databases (e.g., JSTOR, PubMed)
3. Organize literature by themes
4. Analyse findings and identify gaps
5. Summarize with references and citations

Tips for customizing

- Adjust based on specific age groups or mental health issues.
- Follow-up prompts could address tools for organizing references and citations.

Prompt 3: Writing a research report

I need to write a research report on environmental pollution in urban India. Assume that I've collected both qualitative and quantitative data. What sections should be included in the report to ensure it is comprehensive and impactful?

Sample output

1. Executive summary
2. Introduction and research background
3. Methodology (data sources, collection methods)
4. Findings and analysis (graphs, tables for quantitative data)
5. Conclusion and recommendations

Tips for customizing

- Tailor sections based on the specific focus of the research (e.g., air pollution, waste management).
- Include follow-up prompts to format tables and visuals effectively.

Role 4: Mentor

A Mentor provides guidance, support and advice to individuals, particularly students or early-career professionals. They focus on fostering personal and professional growth, often through one-on-one sessions or group mentoring programmes.

Prompt 1: Developing a mentorship plan for college students

I'm creating a mentorship programme for college students in India to help them with career readiness. Assume I need to structure the programme to cover essential skills. What components should be included in the mentorship plan?

Sample output

1. Goal setting and career planning
2. Résumé writing and interview preparation
3. Soft skills development (communication, teamwork)
4. Internship and job search guidance
5. Ongoing evaluation and feedback sessions

Tips for customizing

- Adjust based on specific career fields of the mentees.
- Follow-up prompts can include activity ideas for each component.

Prompt 2: Conducting a mentorship session

I'm about to conduct a mentorship session with a group of high school students. Assume they're interested in science, technology, engineering and mathematics (STEM) careers, but many lack resources. How should I structure the session to inspire and guide them?

Sample output

1. Introduction to STEM fields and career options
2. Sharing real-life success stories in STEM
3. Interactive question and answer (Q&A) session
4. Practical advice on accessible resources and scholarships
5. Goal setting exercise for the next steps

Tips for customizing

- Modify based on the age and academic level of the students.
- Follow-up prompts can focus on suggestions for further STEM exploration.

Prompt 3: Providing feedback to a mentee

One of my mentees is struggling with time management. Assume they're a college student with a busy schedule. How should I approach this feedback session to help them improve?

Sample output

1. Identify specific time management challenges
2. Discuss prioritization techniques (e.g., Eisenhower Matrix)
3. Suggest creating a daily schedule
4. Introduce productivity tools (e.g., planners, apps)
5. Set achievable short-term goals

Tips for customizing

- Customize based on the mentee's course or career demands.

- Follow-up prompts can explore different time management tools for students.

∾

Role 5: Academic Counsellor

An Academic Counsellor provides guidance to students on course selection, career paths and academic challenges. They play an essential role in supporting students' personal and educational growth.

Prompt 1: Guiding a student on course selection

I'm counselling a high school student who is interested in commerce but is unsure about which subjects to choose. Assume the student wants a career in finance or business management. What advice should I give?

Sample output

1. Suggest core subjects (e.g., Accountancy, Business Studies)
2. Recommend electives (e.g., Economics, Entrepreneurship)
3. Discuss benefits of mathematics for finance careers
4. Introduce related co-curricular activities (debate, business clubs)
5. Explore future career options in commerce

Tips for customizing

- Adjust advice based on the specific board curriculum (e.g., CBSE, ICSE).
- Follow-up prompts can address college options and entrance exams for commerce fields.

Prompt 2: Supporting students with exam anxiety

I'm counselling a group of high school students experiencing exam anxiety. Assume the students are preparing for board exams in India. What techniques should I suggest to help them manage anxiety?

Sample output

1. Teach deep breathing and relaxation techniques
2. Encourage regular breaks and a study schedule
3. Promote positive visualization techniques
4. Organize group study or peer support sessions
5. Provide tips on managing time during exams

Tips for customizing

- Customize based on the student's exam board and level of stress.
- Follow-up prompts can delve into long-term stress management practices for students.

Prompt 3: Advising on higher education opportunities

I'm advising a student interested in pursuing engineering in India but unsure about the different entrance exams and universities. What should I explain to them to guide their decision?

Sample output

1. Overview of major entrance exams [e.g., joint entrance examination (JEE), state exams]
2. Discuss top engineering colleges [Indian Institutes of Technology (IITs), National Institutes of Technology (NITs), state universities]
3. Explain different specializations in engineering
4. Guide on preparation tips and resources
5. Information on scholarship opportunities

Tips for customizing

- Modify based on the student's location and field of interest in engineering.

- Follow-up prompts can provide information on specific state-level exams or private universities.

⧜

Role 6: Curriculum Developer

A Curriculum Developer designs educational content, lesson plans and assessments that align with academic standards and cater to students' learning needs. They ensure that curriculum materials are effective, engaging and age-appropriate.

Prompt 1: Designing a science curriculum for primary school

I need to design a science curriculum for primary school students in India. Assume that the focus is on hands-on learning and aligns with CBSE standards. What key elements should I include?

Sample output

1. Basic scientific concepts (e.g., plants, animals, weather)
2. Interactive experiments and hands-on activities
3. Visual learning aids (charts, videos, models)
4. Assessments through projects and quizzes
5. Linking curriculum to environmental awareness

Tips for customizing

- Adjust based on specific grade levels and subjects (e.g., life sciences, earth sciences).
- Follow-up prompts can dive into creating age-appropriate experiment guides.

Prompt 2: Developing digital learning modules

I'm developing digital learning modules for middle school students. Assume that the content is for a mathematics curriculum following the National Council of Educational Research and

Training (NCERT) guidelines. What elements should be included in each module?

Sample output

1. Interactive exercises and quizzes
2. Video lectures or animations for key concepts
3. Practice problems with step by step solutions
4. Self-assessment tools
5. Discussion forum for student queries

Tips for customizing

- Modify based on specific maths topics (e.g., algebra, geometry).
- Follow-up prompts can address tools or software for creating digital content.

Prompt 3: Creating inclusive curriculum for students with special needs

I'm tasked with creating an inclusive curriculum for students with special needs in a mainstream classroom. Assume that the curriculum should be adapted for learning disabilities. What strategies should I include?

Sample output

1. Differentiated instruction techniques
2. Visual and auditory learning tools
3. Incorporation of assistive technology
4. Flexible assessment options
5. Individualized learning goals

Tips for customizing

- Adjust based on specific learning disabilities or challenges.
- Follow-up prompts can focus on techniques for individualizing instruction.

12

Health, Wellness and Caregiving Prompts

Note: Always consult Certified Doctors for every response. This is for reference purposes only.

Role 1: Doctor

A Doctor provides medical care, diagnoses health issues and prescribes treatments. They play a critical role in promoting public health and managing various medical conditions for patients in both urban and rural settings.

Prompt 1: Creating a treatment plan for diabetic patients

I need to create a treatment plan for diabetic patients in a government hospital. Assume that the patients come from diverse socio-economic backgrounds and have limited access to specialized care. What elements should be included in the treatment plan?

Sample output

1. Initial assessment and diagnosis
2. Dietary recommendations and nutrition counselling
3. Medication plan and dosage adjustments
4. Regular monitoring of blood sugar levels
5. Education on lifestyle changes and exercise

Tips for customizing

- Adjust based on the availability of hospital resources and patient demographics.
- Follow-up prompts could focus on creating low-cost dietary plans.

Prompt 2: Conducting a health awareness workshop

I'm organizing a health awareness workshop for rural communities in India. Assume the focus is on common diseases like malaria and dengue. What should I include in the workshop content?

Sample output

1. Overview of symptoms and causes
2. Preventive measures (e.g., mosquito nets, sanitation)
3. First aid tips and when to seek medical help
4. Importance of timely vaccinations and treatments
5. Interactive Q&A session for community members

Tips for customizing

- Modify based on specific regional health issues.
- Follow-up prompts can include preparation of visual aids or handouts.

Prompt 3: Training junior doctors on patient communication

I need to train junior doctors on effective patient communication. Assume the patients are from different cultural and educational backgrounds. What topics should be covered in the training?

Sample output

1. Basics of empathetic listening
2. Clear explanation of diagnosis and treatment
3. Breaking down medical terminology for laypersons
4. Managing difficult conversations (e.g., delivering bad news)

5. Cultural sensitivity in communication

Tips for customizing

- Tailor based on specific departments (e.g., paediatrics, oncology).
- Include follow-up prompts to cover techniques for handling language barriers.

∞

Role 2: Nutritionist

A Nutritionist guides individuals on healthy eating habits, weight management and nutritional requirements. They create personalized dietary plans to promote overall health and wellness.

Prompt 1: Designing a diet plan for pregnant women

I need to design a diet plan for pregnant women attending a government health clinic. Assume that many of these women have limited resources. What should the diet plan include?

Sample output

1. Daily caloric and nutrient requirements
2. Affordable and locally available food options
3. Guidelines for essential vitamins (iron, folic acid)
4. Hydration and meal frequency suggestions
5. Education on foods to avoid during pregnancy

Tips for customizing

- Adjust based on trimester-specific needs.
- Follow-up prompts can focus on creating weekly meal plans.

Prompt 2: Conducting a weight loss workshop

I'm conducting a weight loss workshop for adults in an urban setting. Assume the audience is diverse in terms of fitness levels. What topics should I cover in the workshop?

Sample output

1.   Basics of healthy weight management
2.   Setting realistic weight loss goals
3.   Guidelines on balanced diets and portion control
4.   Introduction to different types of exercise
5.   Tips for sustaining weight loss over time

Tips for customizing

- Modify based on specific age groups or fitness goals.
- Include follow-up prompts for creating handouts on nutrition.

Prompt 3: Providing nutritional advice for diabetic patients

I'm advising a diabetic patient on nutritional habits. Assume the patient is from a rural background with limited access to a variety of foods. What dietary advice should I give?

Sample output

1.   Balanced diet with low glycaemic foods
2.   Encourage high-fibre, wholegrain foods
3.   Limiting sugar and processed foods
4.   Affordable alternatives to common diabetes-friendly foods
5.   Meal frequency and portion control tips

Tips for customizing

- Adjust based on the patient's specific dietary restrictions.
- Follow-up prompts can address lifestyle recommendations for diabetic patients.

Role 3: Physiotherapist

A Physiotherapist helps patients improve their mobility and physical function through exercise, manual therapy and personalized rehabilitation programmes. They work with people recovering from injuries, surgeries and chronic conditions.

Prompt 1: Designing a rehabilitation programme for post surgery patients

I need to design a rehabilitation programme for patients recovering from knee surgery. Assume that the patients vary in age and fitness levels. What should be included in the programme?

Sample output

1.   Initial assessment and baseline testing
2.   Progressive range-of-motion exercises
3.   Strength training for supporting muscles
4.   Guidelines on pain management
5.   Post-rehabilitation home exercise plan

Tips for customizing

- Modify based on the type of knee surgery.
- Include follow-up prompts for examples of specific exercises.

Prompt 2: Educating elderly patients on fall prevention

I'm conducting a session for elderly patients to educate them on fall prevention. Assume the group includes individuals with limited mobility. What topics should I cover?

Sample output

1.   Exercises to improve balance and strength
2.   Home safety tips (lighting, non-slip mats)
3.   Use of assistive devices (canes, walkers)
4.   Proper footwear and clothing

5. Emergency preparedness (who to call, keeping phones accessible)

Tips for customizing

- Adjust based on patient mobility levels.
- Follow-up prompts can address specific exercises for balance.

Prompt 3: Developing a physiotherapy plan for lower back pain

I need to create a physiotherapy plan for a patient with chronic lower back pain. Assume the patient has a sedentary lifestyle. What should the plan include?

Sample output

1. Gentle stretching exercises
2. Strengthening core muscles
3. Posture correction techniques
4. Pain management strategies (heat, cold therapy)
5. Guidance on maintaining activity levels

Tips for customizing

- Modify based on the severity of the pain.
- Include follow-up prompts for recommendations on ergonomic adjustments.

∽

Role 4: Mental Health Counsellor

A Mental Health Counsellor supports individuals dealing with stress, anxiety, depression and other mental health issues. They provide therapeutic techniques, coping mechanisms and a safe space for emotional expression.

Note: Always consult Certified Doctors for every response. This is for reference purposes only.

Prompt 1: Conducting a counselling session for anxiety

I'm conducting a counselling session for a young adult with anxiety. Assume the client is experiencing social anxiety and needs practical techniques for managing it. What should I include in the session?

Sample output

1. Breathing and relaxation exercises
2. Cognitive behavioural techniques for thought reframing
3. Exposure therapy steps for gradual social interaction
4. Journaling and reflective practices
5. Goal setting for social engagement

Tips for customizing

- Adjust based on the client's specific anxiety triggers.
- Follow-up prompts could include techniques for building self-confidence.

Prompt 2: Organizing a workshop on mental health awareness

I'm organizing a mental health awareness workshop for college students. Assume the focus is on stress management and self-care. What topics should be covered?

Sample output

1. Understanding stress and its effects
2. Self-care techniques (e.g., sleep, exercise)
3. Practical stress management tips
4. Recognizing when to seek help
5. Interactive Q&A and resource sharing

Tips for customizing

- Modify based on the student demographic (e.g., engineering students).
- Follow-up prompts can suggest handouts or visual aids for students.

Prompt 3: Providing support for grieving clients

I'm working with a client who recently lost a family member. Assume the client needs support in processing their grief. What steps should I follow during the counselling sessions?

Sample output

1. Allow space for open expression of emotions
2. Normalize grief and discuss stages of grieving
3. Suggest coping strategies (journaling, support groups)
4. Encourage memory sharing and positive reflections
5. Provide resources for continued support

Tips for customizing

- Adjust based on the client's relationship to the deceased.
- Follow-up prompts could focus on long-term grief counselling techniques.

13

Creative Arts, Design and Media Prompts

Role 1: Graphic Designer

A Graphic Designer creates visual concepts and designs logos, layouts and marketing materials to communicate ideas effectively. They work on both digital and print media to support brands and businesses.

Prompt 1: Designing a logo for a start-up

I need to design a logo for a new Indian start-up in the sustainable fashion industry. Assume the brand focuses on eco-friendly and minimalistic styles. What elements should I include in the logo design?

Sample output

1. Nature-inspired colours (greens, earth tones)
2. Minimalist shapes and lines
3. Symbols of sustainability (leaf, recycle icon)
4. Simple typography reflecting elegance
5. Scalable design for various platforms

Tips for customizing

- Adjust based on the start-up's target audience (e.g., youth, eco-conscious consumers).
- Follow-up prompts can explore variations in logo colour schemes.

Prompt 2: Creating a social media post design

I'm designing a social media post for a brand's Independence Day sale. Assume the brand is a mid-range fashion retailer in India. What elements should I include in the design to capture attention?

Sample output

1. Bold, patriotic colours (saffron, white, green)
2. Text overlay for sale details (discount, date)
3. Incorporate Indian cultural motifs (e.g., flag, peacock feathers)
4. Add CTA button (e.g., 'shop now')
5. Use clear and modern font styles

Tips for customizing

- Adjust based on specific target audience preferences.
- Include follow-up prompts for designing carousel posts or stories.

Prompt 3: Designing a product packaging for Indian spices

I need to design packaging for a premium line of Indian spices targeting an international market. Assume the packaging should reflect Indian heritage while looking modern. What design elements should I consider?

Sample output

1. Traditional Indian patterns (paisley, mandalas)
2. Rich, vibrant colours reflecting spice origins
3. Clear typography for product information
4. Eco-friendly packaging materials
5. Illustrations of ingredients or spice origins

Tips for customizing

- Modify based on specific spices or regions (e.g., Kerala spices).
- Follow-up prompts can provide suggestions for branding and colour palettes.

∞

Role 2: Content Writer

A Content Writer produces written content for websites, blogs, social media, and more. They focus on creating engaging, informative and SEO-optimized content tailored to various industries and audiences.

Prompt 1: Writing an SEO-optimized blog post

I need to write an SEO-optimized blog post for a digital marketing agency in India. Assume the topic is 'Top 10 Social Media Trends in India'. What key elements should I include in the post?

Sample output

1. Introduction with relevant keywords
2. List of trends with explanations
3. Data or examples for each trend
4. Call-to-action to engage readers
5. Meta description and alt tags for images

Tips for customizing

- Adjust based on target keywords and audience demographics.
- Follow-up prompts can provide suggestions for internal and external linking.

Prompt 2: Writing a product description for an e-commerce site

I'm writing product descriptions for an Indian e-commerce website selling handcrafted jewellery. Assume the pieces are unique and made by local artisans. What should each description include?

Sample output

1. Highlight unique selling points (e.g., handmade, traditional designs)
2. Material and craft details (e.g., silver, gemstones)
3. Cultural or historical inspiration
4. Emphasis on artisanal quality
5. Size, care instructions and usage suggestions

Tips for customizing

- Adjust based on the specific jewellery style (e.g., temple jewellery, modern fusion).
- Follow-up prompts can suggest variations for SEO-friendly descriptions.

Prompt 3: Creating engaging social media captions

I need to create social media captions for an Indian travel blog's Instagram account. Assume the captions are for a series of posts about hill stations in India. What should I include to make them engaging?

Sample output

1. Highlight the unique charm of each location
2. Incorporate local stories or legends
3. Add a CTA (e.g., 'Tag your travel buddy!')
4. Use relevant hashtags (e.g., #IncredibleIndia, #HillStationVibes)
5. Encourage interaction (e.g., 'Which hill station would you visit next?')

Tips for customizing

- Adjust based on the specific destination or travel theme.
- Include follow-up prompts for creating carousel captions or story scripts.

Role 3: Video Editor

A Video Editor edits footage to create compelling videos for marketing, education, entertainment or other purposes. They focus on visual storytelling, transitions, sound and effects to produce polished videos.

Prompt 1: Editing a promotional video for a restaurant

I need to edit a one-minute promotional video for a new Indian restaurant. Assume the video should showcase the ambience, food and unique dining experience. What elements should I include in the edit?

Sample output

1. Establishing shots of the restaurant's interior
2. Close-ups of signature dishes
3. Voiceover or text overlay describing the experience
4. Background music to match the ambience
5. CTA with contact or location info

Tips for customizing

- Adjust based on the restaurant's theme (e.g., traditional, fusion).
- Follow-up prompts could explore different visual transitions or effects.

Prompt 2: Creating an intro for a YouTube channel

I'm editing a 10-second intro for a YouTube channel focused on

Indian street food. Assume the intro should be engaging and capture the essence of Indian street culture. What should I include?

Sample output

1. Quick shots of popular street foods (pani puri, dosa)
2. Energetic music reflecting Indian street vibes
3. Channel logo animation
4. Text overlays for the channel name and tagline
5. Smooth transition to the main video content

Tips for customizing

- Tailor based on the specific style of the channel.
- Follow-up prompts could provide ideas for logo animation.

Prompt 3: Editing an event highlights video

I need to edit a two-minute highlight video for a wedding in India. Assume the video should capture key moments and be emotional yet vibrant. What should I include in the edit?

Sample output

1. Opening shot of the wedding venue
2. Highlights of key rituals and celebrations
3. Slow-motion shots for emotional moments
4. Background music syncing with the ceremony's energy
5. End shot with the couple's names and wedding date

Tips for customizing

- Adjust based on the cultural background (e.g., North Indian, South Indian wedding).
- Follow-up prompts can explore different music and colour-grading techniques.

Role 4: Social Media Manager

A Social Media Manager handles content creation, scheduling and audience engagement across various platforms. They create strategies to grow online presence, manage brand reputation and connect with followers.

Prompt 1: Planning a monthly content calendar

I need to create a monthly content calendar for an Indian wellness brand on Instagram. Assume the brand focuses on yoga, meditation and natural wellness. What types of posts should I schedule?

Sample output

1. Educational posts (benefits of yoga and meditation)
2. Engagement posts (polls, questions)
3. User-generated content showcasing followers' experiences
4. Weekly wellness tips and guides
5. Promotional posts for products or services

Tips for customizing

- Adjust based on trending wellness topics.
- Include follow-up prompts for hashtags or specific caption ideas.

Prompt 2: Creating an engagement strategy for Facebook

I need to improve engagement on a Facebook page for a local café in India. Assume the page has a small but active following. What engagement strategies should I try?

Sample output

1. Weekly polls or Q&A sessions
2. Behind-the-scenes photos and videos
3. Highlight local events the café is part of

4. Customer spotlights or testimonials
5. Interactive posts (e.g., 'caption this' for food photos)

Tips for customizing

- Modify based on the café's audience demographics.
- Follow-up prompts could suggest ideal posting times for high engagement.

Prompt 3: Managing an influencer collaboration campaign

I'm managing an influencer campaign for an Indian skincare brand. Assume the brand targets millennials interested in natural products. How should I structure the campaign to maximize engagement?

Sample output

1. Select influencers aligned with brand values
2. Define campaign goals (e.g., brand awareness, conversions)
3. Plan content types (tutorials, testimonials, giveaways)
4. Set key performance metrics (likes, shares, comments)
5. Monitor and adjust based on engagement levels

Tips for customizing

- Adjust based on specific influencer types (e.g., beauty bloggers, lifestyle influencers).
- Follow-up prompts could explore techniques for tracking campaign ROI.

14

Human Resources, Training and Development Prompts

Role 1: HR Manager

An HR Manager oversees employee recruitment, engagement and compliance with labour laws. They focus on maintaining a productive work environment, addressing employee concerns and fostering organizational culture.

Prompt 1: Developing an employee onboarding programme

I need to develop an onboarding programme for new hires in a mid-sized tech company in India. Assume the company culture emphasizes innovation and teamwork. What should the programme include?

Sample output

1. Company culture introduction and values
2. Overview of team structure and roles
3. Training sessions on core tools and processes
4. Buddy programme for peer support
5. Performance goals for the first 90 days

Tips for customizing

- Adjust based on department-specific needs (e.g., IT, sales).
- Follow-up prompts can focus on creating interactive onboarding materials.

Prompt 2: Implementing an employee engagement survey

I'm planning an employee engagement survey to improve workplace satisfaction in a large corporate office. Assume the survey should address work–life balance, growth opportunities and team collaboration. What sections should I include?

Sample output

1. Job satisfaction and role fulfilment
2. Work–life balance and flexibility
3. Feedback on leadership and management
4. Opportunities for career growth and learning
5. Overall team dynamics and collaboration

Tips for customizing

- Tailor questions based on company size and structure.
- Follow-up prompts could focus on analysing survey results for actionable insights.

Prompt 3: Creating a policy for remote work

I need to create a remote work policy for employees in an IT company. Assume that the policy should address productivity, communication and data security. What key elements should I include?

Sample output

1. Eligibility and scope of remote work
2. Guidelines for communication and availability
3. Productivity and performance tracking measures
4. Data security and confidentiality requirements
5. Health and wellness support for remote employees

Tips for customizing

- Modify based on the nature of work (e.g., customer support, software development).

- Follow-up prompts can explore specific tools for productivity tracking.

∞

Role 2: Recruitment Specialist

A Recruitment Specialist is responsible for sourcing, screening and hiring talent for various roles within an organization. They create job descriptions, manage the hiring process and ensure a good candidate experience.

Prompt 1: Writing a job description for a sales manager

I need to write a job description for a sales manager in a fast-moving consumer goods (FMCG) company in India. Assume the role requires strong negotiation skills and experience in the Indian market. What should the job description include?

Sample output

1. Role overview and key responsibilities
2. Required skills (e.g., negotiation, communication)
3. Experience needed (e.g., 5+ years in FMCG sales)
4. Educational qualifications
5. Benefits and career growth opportunities

Tips for customizing

- Modify based on target regions or specific industry experience.
- Follow-up prompts can help refine requirements for specific sales channels.

Prompt 2: Developing a candidate screening process

I need to create a candidate screening process for hiring software engineers in a technology company. Assume the goal is to assess both technical and soft skills. What steps should the screening process include?

Sample output

1. Résumé and portfolio review
2. Initial phone screening for culture fit
3. Technical assessment (coding test or project)
4. Behavioural interview to assess soft skills
5. Final round with hiring manager

Tips for customizing

- Adjust based on the specific technical skills required (e.g., Java, Python).
- Follow-up prompts can explore the format of technical assessments.

Prompt 3: Organizing a job fair for campus recruitment

I'm organizing a job fair for campus recruitment at a university in India. Assume the focus is on recruiting engineering and management graduates. What should I include in the event plan?

Sample output

1. Company booths with job information
2. Q&A sessions and panel discussions
3. On-the-spot interview and assessment rounds
4. Networking opportunities with alumni and industry experts
5. Pre-event workshops on résumé writing and interview skills

Tips for customizing

- Adjust based on the specific industries or types of roles being offered.
- Follow-up prompts can help create promotional materials for the event.

⚭

Role 3: Training and Development Specialist

A Training and Development Specialist is responsible for designing and conducting training programmes to upskill employees. They assess learning needs, create instructional content and track training effectiveness.

Prompt 1: Designing a leadership training programme

I need to design a leadership training programme for mid-level managers in a manufacturing company. Assume the focus is on developing decision-making and conflict resolution skills. What topics should I include?

Sample output

1. Decision-making models and tools
2. Effective conflict resolution techniques
3. Communication and feedback skills
4. Emotional intelligence in leadership
5. Team building and motivation strategies

Tips for customizing

- Modify based on industry-specific leadership challenges.
- Follow-up prompts could explore case studies for real-world applications.

Prompt 2: Creating a technical skills training programme

I'm developing a technical skills training programme for entry-level employees in an IT firm. Assume that the programme should cover foundational coding and software development practices. What should I include in the curriculum?

Sample output

1. Introduction to programming languages (e.g., Python, Java)
2. Basics of software development life cycle

3. Debugging and problem-solving techniques
4. Version control basics (e.g., Git)
5. Hands-on projects for practical application

Tips for customizing

- Tailor based on the company's primary tech stack.
- Follow-up prompts can offer suggestions for assessment methods.

Prompt 3: Conducting a time management workshop

I'm conducting a time management workshop for employees in a corporate office. Assume the goal is to improve productivity and reduce stress. What topics should I cover?

Sample output

1. Goal setting and prioritization techniques
2. Effective scheduling and planning
3. Identifying and reducing time wasters
4. Tools for task and time tracking
5. Work–life balance and stress management

Tips for customizing

- Adjust based on specific team functions or time challenges.
- Follow-up prompts could explore group activities to reinforce learning.

Role 4: Employee Relations Specialist

An Employee Relations Specialist focuses on maintaining a positive workplace environment. They handle employee grievances, mediate conflicts and promote open communication within the organization.

Prompt 1: Handling workplace conflicts

I need to address a conflict between two employees in the same team. Assume the conflict is affecting team productivity. What steps should I take to resolve the issue?

Sample output

1. Listen to each employee's perspective
2. Identify the root cause of the conflict
3. Facilitate an open and neutral discussion
4. Agree on a resolution or compromise
5. Follow-up to ensure the issue is resolved

Tips for customizing

- Modify based on specific conflict types (e.g., personal, professional).
- Follow-up prompts could explore methods for tracking resolution effectiveness.

Prompt 2: Conducting employee satisfaction surveys

I need to conduct an employee satisfaction survey in a growing start-up. Assume that the survey will be used to identify workplace improvements. What areas should I include in the survey?

Sample output

1. Job satisfaction and workload
2. Work–life balance and flexibility
3. Opportunities for growth and development
4. Feedback on team and leadership
5. Overall satisfaction and suggestions

Tips for customizing

- Adjust based on the specific company size and industry.
- Follow-up prompts could focus on methods for analysing survey results.

Prompt 3: Developing an employee recognition programme

I'm creating an employee recognition programme to improve morale and productivity. Assume this is for a large corporate setting. What components should the programme include?

Sample output

1. Criteria for recognizing high performers
2. Monthly and quarterly award categories
3. Peer-to-peer recognition opportunities
4. Incentives and benefits for award recipients
5. Public acknowledgement and communication

Tips for customizing

- Tailor based on specific team achievements or performance metrics.
- Follow-up prompts could explore digital platforms for recognition.

Special prompt for deeper résumé evaluation by employers

This prompt is designed to evaluate candidates for specific job roles by thoroughly analysing their résumés and conducting a structured inquiry. The process is tailored for roles such as AI Solution Developer and Sales Manager, ensuring a targeted and professional approach to recruitment. The goal is to:

1. Identify gaps and anomalies in the candidate's résumé based on the job requirements.
2. Ask specific questions to gain insights into their professional experience, technical expertise and role alignment.
3. Document and analyse responses to provide a comprehensive assessment of the candidate's strengths, weaknesses and suitability.

The inquiry includes questions about the candidate's career history, current responsibilities, achievements and expectations, with a focus on real-world project implementation for technical roles or sales metrics for sales-related roles.

The final output delivers a detailed evaluation with recommendations, enabling an informed decision-making process aligned with organizational goals. The HR person may attach the report to the candidate's résumé to make it easy for evaluators.

Prompt

We are considering this candidate for the following job role: AI Solution Developer

Key objectives of the prompt

1. Identify negatives in the résumé relative to the job role and any anomalies.
2. Conduct a detailed inquiry based on the following questions, ensuring responses are documented and included as part of the final report:
   - Reasons for leaving the last three companies (provide company name and tenure in years for reference).
   - Why is the candidate leaving the current job?
   - What is the current CTC and current take-home salary?
   - What is the team size reporting to him?
   - Has the candidate been informed about the company's policy of the same salary with a three-month review?
   - What salary is the candidate expecting (same as current or with a percentage increase)?

Process to follow:

1. Ask one question at a time, wait for my answer and proceed step by step.
2. Do not create the final report until all answers are received.
3. Compare the candidate's LinkedIn profile (if available) with

the résumé, and highlight any discrepancies or additional insights in a separate note.

Final output:

- Present a comprehensive analysis of the candidate's strengths, weaknesses and suitability for the role.
- Include all responses to the above questions in the final report.
- Conclude with an expert opinion on whether to proceed with the candidate's application based on the findings.

You can display basic information about candidates and start by asking questions. Don't show me the entire process in detail. Ensure the process is professional, detailed and aligned with expert recruitment standards.

Additional questions based on role

The following question is for candidates applying to sales roles.

- How many people from your team were typically involved in the sales cycle?
- What was the biggest order closed in the last year, and what was its value?

The following question is for AI profile candidates:

- Have you done any project on AI which is live and accessible on the internet?

Comprehensive career advancement prompts for job seekers

1. Crafting impactful résumés for job applications

Instructions: Upload your existing résumé or provide details about your work experience, skills and accomplishments to create or revise a professional résumé.

Prompts

- Help me create a résumé for a [specific job role] in [industry/sector], focusing on measurable achievements, relevant skills and industry-specific language.
- Revise my résumé to include action-oriented language and quantify accomplishments to make it more impactful for hiring managers.
- Optimize my résumé for Applicant Tracking System (ATS) by ensuring it includes relevant keywords and formats for [specific job role].
- Design a visually appealing résumé layout for a creative role in [industry/sector], ensuring it stands out while maintaining professionalism.
- Analyse successful résumés in [specific field] and recommend elements or strategies I can adopt to improve my own.

2. Strategic networking for career advancement

Instructions: Provide your LinkedIn profile link or describe your target industry and networking goals to create personalized strategies.

Prompts

- Create a personalized networking script for reaching out to professionals in [industry/sector] on LinkedIn to build meaningful connections.
- Develop a detailed strategy for maximizing networking opportunities at events and conferences related to [industry/field].
- Provide step by step instructions on leveraging alumni or professional networks for career advancement in [specific industry].
- Guide me on how to use social media effectively to establish a professional brand in [industry/role].

- Write a cold outreach email template for contacting industry leaders to seek advice or job referrals in [field/role].

3. Navigating career transitions with confidence

Instructions: Share your current job role, desired career field and skills you'd like to transfer for a detailed transition plan.

Prompts

- Develop a step by step guide to transition from [current role/industry] to [new role/industry], highlighting transferable skills and a clear action plan.
- Identify certifications or training programmes that will help me bridge skill gaps and prepare for a career change to [new field].
- Draft a compelling cover letter explaining my career switch to [new field], emphasizing my strengths and potential contributions.
- Help me reframe my work experience to appeal to recruiters in [new field] by focusing on transferable skills and achievements.
- Suggest strategies to manage financial and emotional challenges during a career transition, including setting realistic timelines.

4. Mastering salary negotiation for better compensation

Instructions: Share your current salary, job role and expected compensation for personalized negotiation strategies.

Prompts

- Draft a salary negotiation script tailored for [SPECIFIC ROLE] at [company], emphasizing my value and current market trends.

- Help me prepare data-driven arguments for negotiating my salary, including market benchmarks for [role] in [industry/location].
- Suggest responses for handling difficult questions about compensation expectations during job interviews for [specific role].
- Write a professional follow-up email to revisit salary discussions after an interview, reinforcing my qualifications and expectations.
- Develop a framework to evaluate job offers holistically, considering salary, benefits, career growth, and work–life balance.

5. Excelling in job interviews

Instructions: Share details about the job role, company, and industry to create tailored interview preparation strategies.

Prompts

- Generate a list of common interview questions and ideal responses tailored for [specific job role] in [industry/sector].
- Create a mock interview script focused on technical and behavioural questions for a [specific role].
- Provide strategies for addressing sensitive topics, like career gaps, during an interview for [role].
- Help me craft a compelling answer to 'Tell me about yourself', tailored for an interview in [industry/role].
- Write a professional post-interview thank-you email that reiterates my enthusiasm for the position and highlights key discussion points.

6. Understanding job market trends and opportunities

Instructions: Specify the industry, job role and location you want analysed to generate relevant insights and trends.

- Conduct an analysis of job market trends in [specific industry], identifying high-demand roles and the necessary skills for the next five years.
- Identify emerging skills in [field] and suggest actionable steps to acquire these skills for career growth.
- Compare job opportunities in [specific region/industry], highlighting potential career growth, challenges and salaries.
- Analyse the impact of technological advancements on career prospects in [field/role] and recommend ways to stay competitive.
- Investigate regional job market differences for [industry/role] and suggest the best locations for pursuing opportunities.

7. Planning your professional development journey

Instructions: Share your career goals, areas for improvement and feedback from past evaluations for a customized growth plan.

Prompts

- Create a personalized career development plan, including short-term and long-term goals for advancing in [industry/role].
- Recommend certifications, training programmes or degrees that can enhance my expertise in [specific field].
- Analyse feedback from past performance reviews and outline actionable steps for improving critical professional skills.
- Suggest ways to integrate my personal interests with professional goals to maintain work–life balance and long-term satisfaction.
- Provide a list of professional organizations or forums I should join to grow my network and learn in [specific field].

15

Operations, Supply Chain and Logistics Prompts

Role 1: Supply Chain Manager

A Supply Chain Manager oversees the end-to-end movement of goods, ensuring cost efficiency, timely delivery and adherence to quality standards. They manage relationships with suppliers, coordinate logistics and implement strategies to optimize the supply chain. Due to India's diverse geography and infrastructure, they often need to adapt strategies to navigate challenges such as transportation delays, supplier constraints and regional regulatory requirements.

Prompt 1: Optimizing supplier management for cost efficiency

I need to optimize supplier management for a mid-sized manufacturing company in India to reduce costs without compromising quality. Assume that we rely on local suppliers for raw materials and face frequent price fluctuations. What actions should I take to manage costs effectively?

Sample output

1. Negotiating long-term contracts with fixed pricing
2. Implementing a vendor performance evaluation system
3. Building a diversified supplier network
4. Conducting regular cost audits
5. Using bulk ordering discounts

Tips for customizing

- Tailor based on the specific industry (e.g., FMCG, automotive).
- Include follow-up prompts to focus on vendor-specific challenges, such as quality issues or delivery delays.

Advanced prompt

Using predictive analytics and data from previous supply chain cycles, I want to build a forecasting model to proactively adjust sourcing strategies for seasonal price fluctuations and regional supply disruptions. Assume I need to factor in past supplier performance, transportation delays and external market trends. What steps should I take to develop this forecasting model?

Prompt 2: Managing inventory for optimal stock levels

I need to improve inventory management for a retail company in India to avoid stockouts and overstocking. Assume that demand varies seasonally, and storage space is limited. What strategies should I implement?

Sample output

1. Implementing just-in-time (JIT) inventory
2. Setting reorder points based on demand forecasts
3. Using ABC analysis for inventory prioritization
4. Regular cycle counts and audits
5. Collaborating with suppliers for faster restocking

Tips for customizing

- Adjust strategies based on product types or high-demand seasons.
- Follow-up prompts could explore specific software options for inventory tracking.

Advanced prompt

Develop a dynamic inventory optimization model that integrates historical sales data, seasonal demand trends and real-time supplier availability. What algorithms or tools can be used to implement a responsive and predictive inventory system?

Prompt 3: Reducing transportation costs in the supply chain

Our company faces high transportation costs for shipping goods across multiple states in India. Assume the goal is to reduce these costs while maintaining delivery timelines. What steps should I consider?

Sample output

1. Optimize route planning for efficient delivery
2. Negotiate volume discounts with carriers
3. Use regional warehousing to minimize long-distance shipments
4. Invest in fuel-efficient or electric vehicles (if feasible)
5. Collaborate with other businesses for shared transportation

Tips for customizing

- Adjust based on product type (e.g., perishable versus non-perishable).
- Follow-up prompts could focus on route optimization tools or software.

Advanced prompt

Analyse transportation costs across different carriers and routes using historical delivery data to develop a cost-minimization model. Assume the model should account for fuel price fluctuations, peak traffic hours and potential toll costs. What data inputs and model frameworks would be ideal for this analysis?

∽

Role 2: Operations Manager

An Operations Manager oversees daily business operations, focusing on efficiency, cost control and quality management. They work to streamline processes, manage resources and ensure smooth coordination across departments to meet organizational goals.

Prompt 1: Streamlining operational processes for efficiency

I need to streamline operational processes in a manufacturing plant to reduce waste and improve productivity. Assume the plant produces consumer goods and is looking to increase output without increasing costs. What steps should I take?

Sample output

1. Implement lean manufacturing principles
2. Automate repetitive processes where feasible
3. Conduct time-and-motion studies to identify bottlenecks
4. Train staff on best practices for efficiency
5. Do regular process reviews to identify improvement areas

Tips for customizing

- Tailor based on the specific manufacturing processes involved.
- Follow-up prompts could explore particular lean methodologies (e.g., Kaizen, Six Sigma).

Advanced prompt

Design a data-driven process optimization plan using real-time production data, aiming to minimize downtime and increase output. How should I structure this plan, and which performance metrics and tools will be most effective?

Prompt 2: Improving workplace safety standards

Our factory in India needs to improve its safety standards to comply with national regulations and reduce workplace accidents. Assume that we employ a large workforce with varied educational backgrounds. What steps should I implement?

Sample output

1. Conduct a workplace safety audit
2. Implement safety training programmes for all employees
3. Install clear safety signage and emergency exits
4. Introduce regular safety drills and inspections
5. Set up a reporting system for safety incidents

Tips for customizing

- Adjust based on the specific hazards of the industry (e.g., heavy machinery, chemical use).
- Follow-up prompts could explore methods for measuring the effectiveness of safety protocols.

Advanced prompt

Create a safety compliance programme that incorporates predictive analytics to identify high-risk areas and potential incidents. What data sources, analytics tools and risk indicators should I prioritize?

Prompt 3: Managing resource allocation during peak demand

I need to manage resource allocation for a seasonal increase in demand for our product in India. Assume that resources are limited and include personnel, machinery and storage. What strategies should I employ?

Sample output

1. Forecast demand and then schedule resources
2. Implement shift adjustments and overtime for staff
3. Prioritize high-demand product lines for production
4. Utilize temporary storage solutions

5. Collaborate with third-party vendors for additional capacity

Tips for customizing

- Tailor based on specific peak seasons or regions in India.
- Follow-up prompts could address hiring temporary staff or acquiring rental equipment.

Advanced prompt

Develop a resource allocation model that dynamically adjusts based on real-time demand fluctuations, seasonal forecasts and current resource availability. How should I set up this model, and what algorithms would be best for responsive adjustments?

∞

Role 3: Logistics Coordinator

A Logistics Coordinator manages the movement and storage of goods from suppliers to customers. They ensure timely deliveries, track shipments and coordinate with warehouses and transportation providers to avoid delays or stockouts.

Prompt 1: Coordinating multi-location shipments for timely delivery

I need to coordinate shipments across multiple locations in India to ensure timely delivery. Assume that each location has different delivery timelines and transportation constraints. What steps should I follow?

Sample output

1. Develop a shipment schedule based on delivery deadlines
2. Use route optimization tools for efficient paths
3. Coordinate with local transport providers for regional expertise

4. Monitor real-time tracking and adjust routes if needed
5. Communicate proactively with each location for updates

Tips for customizing

- Modify based on specific types of products (e.g., perishables versus non-perishables).
- Follow-up prompts could explore software for real-time tracking.

Advanced prompt

Create a route optimization model that incorporates real-time traffic data, regional transport restrictions and warehouse availability to ensure timely multi-location delivery. What algorithms and data sources would support efficient route planning?

Prompt 2: Managing warehouse space for seasonal products

Our company needs to manage limited warehouse space during a seasonal increase in product demand. Assume the products are consumer goods of varying sizes. What strategies should I implement?

Sample output

1. Prioritize high-demand stock-keeping units (SKUs) and optimize space usage
2. Implement JIT inventory for less popular items
3. Use vertical storage solutions for maximum capacity
4. Outsource overflow storage to nearby warehouses if needed
5. Conduct regular inventory checks to free up space

Tips for customizing

- Adjust based on product dimensions and warehouse layout.
- Follow-up prompts could include space optimization software recommendations.

Advanced prompt

Develop a warehouse space optimization strategy using demand forecasting and inventory turnover rates to ensure space availability during peak seasons. How should I set up this strategy, and what data should I collect?

Prompt 3: Reducing shipping delays for e-commerce orders

I need to reduce shipping delays for e-commerce orders to improve customer satisfaction in India. Assume the delays are primarily due to last-mile delivery issues. What solutions should I consider?

Sample output

1. Partner with reliable last-mile delivery providers
2. Optimize packaging for faster sorting and delivery
3. Use regional distribution centres for faster fulfilment
4. Implement real-time tracking for customers
5. Offer flexible delivery options (express, standard, etc.)

Tips for customizing

- Tailor solutions based on specific regions (e.g., urban versus rural).
- Follow-up prompts could explore customer feedback on delivery experience.

Advanced prompt

Design a predictive model to identify and mitigate last-mile delivery delays based on historical data, traffic patterns and regional bottlenecks. What inputs and algorithms should I prioritize for maximum efficiency?

16

Wellness, Personal Growth and Lifestyle Prompts

This category focuses on roles dedicated to enhancing individuals' physical, mental and emotional well-being. Practitioners in this category—such as life coaches, meditation trainers and yoga instructors—guide clients through personal growth journeys, helping them to cultivate resilience, mindfulness and a balanced lifestyle.

Rooted in techniques that often draw from India's rich cultural heritage in wellness, this category emphasizes both traditional practices and modern approaches to support holistic health, stress management and personal development. Each role offers tailored methods to meet diverse client needs, creating accessible and sustainable paths towards self-improvement and wellness.

Note: AI should be used as a supporting tool and cannot replace actual knowledge, skill and training. Not everyone using it can become a life coach or counsellor.

∞

Role 1: Life Coach

A Life Coach assists clients with personal and professional growth, focusing on setting goals, building self-confidence and overcoming challenges. They guide clients through actionable steps to achieve a balanced and fulfilling life, often using culturally relevant approaches that resonate within the Indian context.

Prompt 1: Helping clients set personal goals

A client is struggling to set achievable personal goals and feels overwhelmed. Assume they are looking to improve their work–life balance, health and self-confidence. How should I guide the client in setting realistic and motivating goals?

Sample output

1. Identify specific areas for improvement and break down goals
2. Encourage the use of SMART goals (specific, measurable, achievable, relevant, time-bound)
3. Guide in setting short-term and long-term goals
4. Create a visual goal-tracking system (journals, charts)
5. Plan regular check-ins to adjust goals as needed

Tips for customizing

- Tailor based on the client's immediate priorities and lifestyle.
- Include follow-up prompts to explore goal-setting tools like vision boards or habit trackers.

Advanced prompt

As a Life Coach, design a personalized goal-setting framework for clients who need assistance with prioritizing life goals. Consider the following elements:

1. **Role:** As a supportive coach, guide clients to clarify their values and define achievable steps towards long-term aspirations.
2. **Scope:** The framework should focus on practical goal-setting methods that improve work–life balance, health and self-confidence.

3. **Boundaries:** Avoid setting goals too quickly; help clients explore their motivations and capabilities over several sessions for sustainable commitment.
4. **Expertise:** Leverage culturally relatable practices, such as journaling or using affirmations rooted in mindfulness, which can help clients remain grounded.
5. **Specifics:** Structure the framework to introduce SMART goals, daily reflections and weekly assessments, encouraging clients to create visual aids like charts or trackers.
6. **Tone:** Keep a motivational and empathetic tone, helping clients embrace progress while handling setbacks calmly and constructively.'

Prompt 2: Improving self-confidence in clients

A client feels a lack of self-confidence, especially in social situations. Assume they struggle with self-doubt and have faced criticism in the past. What steps should I take to help them build self-confidence gradually?

Sample output

1. Identify and challenge limiting beliefs
2. Encourage self-compassion and positive self-talk
3. Introduce gradual social exposure exercises
4. Set small, achievable confidence goals
5. Practise reflection on positive experiences

Tips for customizing

- Adjust based on the client's specific experiences and social goals.
- Include follow-up prompts to develop self-affirmation exercises.

Advanced prompt

Develop a confidence-building programme for clients with self-doubt issues. The programme should address the following:

1. **Role:** As a life coach, provide a nurturing space that allows clients to identify and challenge self-limiting beliefs.
2. **Scope:** Focus the programme on foundational self-confidence exercises with gradual social exposure practices.
3. **Boundaries:** Avoid overwhelming clients by setting manageable steps; encourage progression based on individual comfort.
4. **Expertise:** Incorporate cognitive behavioural techniques (CBT) for reframing negative thoughts, emphasizing compassion.
5. **Specifics:** Establish small goals, such as initiating conversations or public speaking exercises, tailored to client comfort.
6. **Tone:** Maintain an encouraging and compassionate tone, reinforcing every positive step to foster resilience and self-assurance.

∞

Role 2: Meditation Trainer

A Meditation Trainer in India helps clients improve mental clarity and reduce stress through meditation techniques. They guide clients of various backgrounds and experience levels, using culturally resonant practices to support relaxation and self-awareness.

Prompt 1: Creating a beginner meditation programme

I need to design a beginner-friendly meditation programme for clients who have no prior experience with meditation. Assume the goal is to help them relax and improve focus gradually over time. What elements should I include in the programme to ensure accessibility and consistency?

Sample output

1. Introduction to basic meditation principles

2. Short, guided sessions focused on breathing techniques
3. Simple mindfulness exercises for daily practice
4. Weekly progress reviews and adjustments
5. Encouragement to maintain a journal of reflections

Tips for customizing

- Tailor based on client age, time availability and desired outcomes.
- Include follow-up prompts to explore advanced techniques as clients progress.

Advanced prompt

Develop a structured meditation programme for beginners using the following elements:

1. **Role:** As a trainer, provide foundational guidance on mindfulness, focus and relaxation techniques.
2. **Scope:** Limit the programme to 4–6 weeks, emphasizing short daily sessions to establish a meditation habit.
3. **Boundaries:** Avoid complex techniques or advanced practices; focus solely on accessible, beginner-friendly meditations
4. **Expertise:** Integrate culturally relevant techniques, such as breathing practices like Nadi Shodhana and visualizations.
5. **Specifics:** Outline weekly objectives with specific exercises, gradually increasing session duration from 5 to 15 minutes.
6. **Tone:** Maintain a calming and supportive tone to reassure clients, encouraging self-compassion as they learn.

Prompt 2: Leading a group meditation session

I'm leading a group meditation session for corporate employees in India. Assume they are new to meditation and have high-stress jobs. How should I structure the session to ensure relaxation and engagement?

1. Begin with a brief introduction on meditation benefits
2. Guide through basic breathing techniques
3. Use a simple body-scan exercise for relaxation
4. Encourage mindfulness of the present moment
5. Close with reflection and feedback

Tips for customizing

- Adjust session duration based on group time constraints.
- Include follow-up prompts to create meditation resources for employees.

Advanced prompt

Design a guided meditation programme for a corporate setting, focusing on stress relief and mindfulness. Consider these elements:

1. **Role:** As a meditation trainer, facilitate a calming space for employees to unwind and reconnect.
2. **Scope:** Limit sessions to 20–30 minutes, focusing on simple relaxation exercises suitable for busy professionals.
3. **Boundaries:** Avoid complex visualizations or spiritual practices; keep the meditation techniques secular and workplace-friendly
4. **Expertise:** Use breathing and body-scan techniques known for reducing stress, aligning with the professional environment.
5. **Specifics:** Structure the programme to begin with breathing exercises, progressing to mindfulness of physical sensations, with light, calming background music.
6. **Tone:** Maintain a grounding and supportive tone, helping participants leave the session refreshed and motivated.

Role 3: Yoga Trainer

A Yoga Trainer guides clients through yoga practices to improve physical health, flexibility and mental well-being. They design routines suitable for various fitness levels, using techniques that promote holistic wellness.

Prompt 1: Designing a yoga routine for beginners

I need to create a yoga routine for beginners focusing on flexibility and stress relief. Assume the clients are not physically active. What exercises should I include to help them ease into yoga?

Sample output

1. Introduce gentle warm-up movements
2. Guide through basic poses like cat-cow and child's pose
3. Incorporate breathing techniques for relaxation
4. End with a short meditation or Shavasana
5. Encourage regular practice for gradual improvement

Tips for customizing

- Adjust based on clients' physical limitations.
- Include follow-up prompts for creating advanced sequences as flexibility improves.

Advanced prompt

Develop a yoga training routine for beginners focusing on flexibility and stress management, using the following guidelines:

1. **Role:** As a yoga trainer, create a safe and nurturing space to encourage mindful movement and relaxation.
2. **Scope:** Focus on beginner-friendly poses and slow transitions, targeting core flexibility and stress reduction.
3. **Boundaries:** Avoid challenging poses; limit the practice to low-impact stretches and relaxation techniques.

4. **Expertise:** Leverage popular Indian yoga techniques like Pranayama (breathing) to promote relaxation and mindfulness.

5. **Specifics:** Structure sessions with a warm-up, followed by 5–6 gentle asanas, concluding with breathing exercises and Shavasana.

6. **Tone:** Keep a soothing and empowering tone, reminding clients that progress is gradual and celebrating small achievements.

Bonus prompts for general use

These prompts are designed to simplify everyday tasks by transforming images into actionable insights. Whether it's transcribing notes, diagnosing technical issues, planning meals, improving style or home décor, optimizing social media profiles or organizing brainstorming ideas, these prompts help users streamline their workflow, save time and make informed decisions easily.

1. Find product alternatives

Take a picture of a product you have and use this prompt: Suggest affordable or better alternatives to this product available in India. Include options available in nearby stores or online, with a focus on quality and cost-effectiveness.

2. Quickly diagnose technical issues

If something's broken, like a gadget or device, snap a picture of it and use this prompt: Based on this image, identify the problem and give me step by step instructions to fix it. Let me know if I can handle it myself or if I need to call a professional.

3. Plan meals from what's in your fridge

Take a picture of the ingredients in your fridge or pantry and use this prompt: Create a meal plan for the week using these ingredients for breakfast, lunch and dinner. Include simple recipes that help me avoid extra trips to the store and focus on healthy, quick-to-make meals.

4. Get fashion advice

Take a picture of your outfit or wardrobe and use this prompt: Give me feedback on my outfit or wardrobe and suggest how I can improve my style. Offer tips on fit, colour coordination, and how to mix and match pieces for different occasions. Also, recommend affordable options to upgrade my look.

5. Improve your home décor

Take a picture of a room in your home and use this prompt: Analyse the design of this room and suggest ways to improve its style or function. Recommend new furniture arrangements, colour schemes and lighting changes. If possible, include affordable upgrades or DIY ideas.

6. Optimize your social media profile

Take a screenshot of your social media profile or a recent post and use this prompt: Review my profile, including my bio and recent posts, and suggest ways to improve it for better engagement. Provide tips on how to improve the look, content strategy, hashtags and the best times to post.

7. Identify a landmark or object

Take a picture of a landmark, artwork or an unfamiliar object and use this prompt: Based on this image, identify the landmark or object and give me some interesting facts or historical background about it.

8. Turn brainstorm ideas into a to-do list

Take a picture of your brainstorming session or whiteboard notes and use this prompt: Turn the information in this image into an organized to-do list. Prioritize the tasks, assign deadlines if necessary and make each task actionable for easy follow-through.

9. Instantly transcribe handwritten notes

If you have handwritten notes, a whiteboard or brainstorming ideas, take a picture and use this prompt: Transcribe the content from this image into clear, organized notes. Break it down by sections or topics, and convert any diagrams into simple text. Make the notes easy to review and fit into my existing format.

Bonus prompts: Hours of work in seconds

1. Summarize long documents (tender, gazette, book, technical documents, etc.)

Read this [insert link or upload document] and provide a detailed summary highlighting the main points, conclusions and any recommendations.

2. Generate reports from data

Generate a comprehensive report from the attached spreadsheet data, focusing on key metrics like sales growth, customer acquisition costs and profit margins over the last quarter.

3. Draft professional emails

Write a professional email to [recipient's name] regarding [subject matter], ensuring to cover all key points such as [key point 1], [key point 2] and [key point 3].

4. Create PowerPoint presentations

Design a PowerPoint presentation based on the contents of the provided document. Include slides for introduction, key findings, data analysis and conclusion.

5. Draft legal documents

Draft a basic [type of contract, e.g., non-disclosure agreement] for a partnership between [Company A] and [Company B], specifying key terms such as confidentiality, duration and obligations of each party.

6. Convert meeting notes into actionable tasks

Here are my meeting notes [insert notes]. Can you organize these into a clear list of actionable tasks with assigned team members and deadlines?

7. Marketing plan

- Draft a social media post for [new product/service] using the four Cs (clear, concise, compelling and credible) framework to ensure engagement.
- Create an Instagram post for [new product/service] using storytelling to connect with the audience emotionally with CTA.
- Write a Twitter/X thread on 'How to make an Instagram reel that can go viral' using the HERO framework (hook, empathy, response and overcome) to capture attention and drive interaction.

17

AI-Generated Images: A Game Changer

AI-generated visuals are changing the ways brand managers, marketers and creative professionals bring ideas to life. What earlier took weeks because of discussions among members of the design team and approvals can now happen in minutes. With the help of AI, you can visualize brand directions, explore multiple creative options and get design-ready visuals that align with your brand—all without needing to open Photoshop or hire a designer.

The magic lies in how smart these tools have become. You give them a prompt, and they interpret it with context. Whether it's packaging mock-ups, product illustrations or full branding sheets, AI tools are now producing results that are presentation-ready, fast and on-brand.

Where AI-generated images work best

Here are a few places where I've found AI imagery to be incredibly useful:

1. **Rapid prototyping:** Want to see five versions of your new product packaging? Just describe it. AI gives you visual directions instantly so you can explore, refine or pivot—without spending days on mock-ups.
2. **Brand concept visualization:** Founders and designers can quickly create mood boards, layout styles or logo variations to test ideas before taking them to full design.
3. **Marketing and campaign visuals:** Need a quick visual

for a social media post or product feature? AI can generate on-brand creatives that fit right into your content calendar.

4. **Client and investor presentations:** Want to impress a client or pitch your next big idea? Use AI visuals to show your vision clearly—without waiting on design revisions.
5. **Localization for different markets:** AI allows you to adapt visuals for various cultures, regions or languages, helping you connect with the right audience while keeping the brand identity intact.
6. **Saves time and cuts costs:** Skip the expensive photo shoots or design delays. With AI, your marketing team can work faster and more creatively, often with better results.

To show how all this comes together, I am taking the example of Scooter, a traditional Indian brand known for its Agmark Grade 1 Kachchi Ghani Mustard Oil. By using AI-generated branding assets—such as logo treatments, packaging mock-ups and lifestyle illustrations—it's possible to retain the brand's cultural flavour while updating its visuals to meet the expectations of the modern consumer.

Designing AI-enhanced brand identity sheets

As AI continues to reshape the marketing and branding landscape, the importance of presenting a cohesive and futuristic brand identity becomes even more vital. In this chapter, we explore how AI can aid in the development of brand identity sheets, with a specific focus on visual clarity, smart layout and contextual adaptation for diverse industries.

We'll walk through an example of how a traditional consumer brand like 'Scooter'—known for its Kachchi Ghani Mustard Oil—can embrace AI-generated visual branding to maintain cultural roots while adopting modern design standards. You are encouraged to modify these prompts for your own products and services.

Task 1: AI-generated brand sheet— Scooter Mustard Oil

Prompt

Create a modern vertical brand identity overview sheet for Scooter—Kachchi Ghani Mustard Oil, showcasing all key brand design elements in a structured, clean and visually rich layout. The sheet should be designed for internal brand reference and marketing alignment. The layout should be vertically stacked modules or cards (not bento boxes), with clear section labels and a visually pleasing, contemporary Indian FMCG aesthetic. The tone should reflect trust, purity, heritage and health, while still being fresh and appealing to modern consumers.

Sections to include (from top to bottom)

1. **Logo**
   - » Display the Scooter brand logo prominently.
   - » Include a short caption: The trusted taste of purity— since [founding year].
   - » Show the logo in full colour and also on a white/ light background for usage reference.
2. **Colour palette**
   - » Present four core brand colours in clean rectangular swatches with HEX codes:
     - ◦ Mustard yellow: #F4B400 (purity, vitality)
     - ◦ Deep red: #B5121B (richness, tradition)
     - ◦ Leaf green: #4CAF50 (natural, healthy)
     - ◦ Pure white: #FFFFFF (cleanliness, simplicity)
   - » Label the section clearly: Colour Palette

3. **Typography**
   » Choose legible and expressive fonts:
     ◦ Heading font: Poppins Bold (modern yet approachable)
     ◦ Body font: Mukta Regular (readability + clean look)
   » Show sample text like:
     ◦ Pure Kachchi Ghani Mustard Oil
     ◦ For every Indian kitchen, since decades
4. **Gradients**
   » Display two warm and rich gradient examples:
     ◦ Gradient 1: Mustard yellow → Deep red
     ◦ Gradient 2: Leaf green → Light yellow
   » Caption: Used across packaging, digital banners and print
5. **Icons**
   » Show six minimal icons in brand colours:
     ◦ Healthy heart, cooking pot, drop of oil, factory, AGMARK seal, Indian bay leaf
   » Design style: Flat, bold-line icons with colour accents
6. **Illustrations**
   » A lifestyle illustration or creative photo-style graphic:
     ◦ A happy Indian woman cooking with mustard oil, or
     ◦ The mustard oil pouch with flowing aroma lines and a '100% purity' badge
   » Style: Modern Indian + FMCG packaging blend
   » Label the section: Illustration

Style guidelines

- **Orientation:** Vertical, A3 size or 1080×1920px
- **Design style:** Clean, vibrant, culturally rooted, FMCG-forward

- **Containers:** Rounded corners (8px), light shadows [e.g., rgba(0, 0, 0, 0.08)]
- **Background:** Light off-white or pale yellow for warmth (#FFFBEA)
- **Typography hierarchy:** Headings (32px), subheads (22px), body (16px)
- **Spacing:** Balanced white space, clear visual separation
- **Overall tone:** Trustworthy, natural and Indian household-friendly

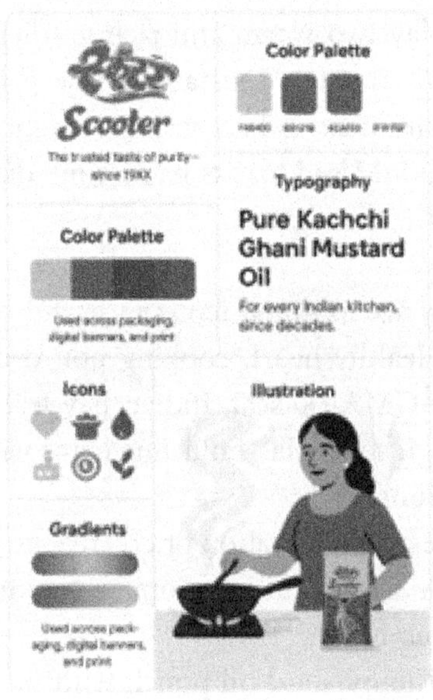

How AI enables this

Using AI tools like text-to-image generation, creative teams can instantly visualize brand mood boards, packaging concepts and layout guides without needing to manually illustrate or design from scratch. This unlocks faster iterations, design standardization and easy adaptation across product categories.

Task 2: Social media promotion image

Note: The following images have been used for illustration purposes only. These belong to the respective owner of the logo/ trademark.

We need to upload our desired images to an AI tool (say, ChatGPT). The above images were uploaded and used to produce the final image.

Prompt

Using all uploaded images, create a high-resolution digital photo of a young Indian woman with a bright smile, standing in a modern Indian kitchen. She is wearing a yellow sari and holding a pouch of Scooter Kachchi Ghani Mustard Oil with both hands, close to her chest. Use Scooter and AGMARK logo as a running pattern on her yellow sari.

Task 3: Use templates to create new designs

Templates

<table>
<tr>
<td>

HIGH-QUALITY PRODUCT IMAGE ON WHITE BACKGROUND

Showcase a clear, distraction-free image of your product on a plain white background to highlight its design, packaging.

</td>
<td>

PRODUCT BEING USED IN REAL–LIFE CONTEXT

Demonstrate the product in action — e.g., being applied, poured, consumed, or worn — to build relatability and show practical use.

</td>
<td>

TOP 3 PRODUCT BENEFITS WITH VISUALS

List three strong benefits or USPs (e.g. organic ingredients, long-lasting, improves skin tone) while keeping the product in the frame.

</td>
</tr>
<tr>
<td>

HUMAN ELEMENT – HAND OR MODEL HOLDING THE PRODUCT

Include a hand or full model to show scale, trust, and connect emotionally with the audience. Brand

</td>
<td>

CUSTOMER TESTIMONIAL– USER-GENERATED STYLE

Show a real quote or feedback from a user. Use casual tone and smartphone-style visual to replicate UGC (User Generated Ct).

</td>
<td>

CLOSE-UP SHOT OF PRODUCT TEXTURE / DETAILS

Zoom in on product texture, ingredients, color, craftsmanship or packaging details to reinforce quality and sensory appeal.

</td>
</tr>
</table>

Prompt

Use this template and create an advertisement image for Katrina Biscuits. Don't reproduce text in the template on the advertisement images. Use all sections of the template to generate new images.

Output

18

Prompts for Emerging Technologies

As the digital landscape evolves, new technologies such as Internet of Things (IoT), blockchain, augmented reality (AR)/ virtual reality (VR), and autonomous systems are reshaping industries and daily life. The ability to interact seamlessly with these technologies through effective prompt engineering is crucial for staying ahead in this rapidly advancing era. This chapter explores how prompts can unlock the potential of these cutting-edge technologies, empowering users to drive innovation and efficiency.

1. IoT: Crafting smart prompts for connected devices

IoT connects devices, sensors and systems to enable smarter environments. Effective prompts for IoT can enhance automation, data insights and real-time decision-making.

Example prompts

1. **For smart homes:** Design a daily schedule for my smart home that optimizes energy usage while maintaining comfort during summers in Jaipur.
2. **For predictive maintenance:** Generate a report analysing anomalies in sensor data from factory machinery over the past month.
3. **For environmental monitoring:** Identify patterns in

air quality sensor readings across Delhi to recommend pollution-reducing strategies.[7]

Advanced prompt

Integrate data from IoT devices (temperature, motion and energy consumption) to create an energy efficiency strategy for a 100-room hotel. The solution should balance guest comfort with cost savings and environmental impact.

2. Blockchain: Prompts for transparency and efficiency

Blockchain technology enables secure, decentralized transactions. Effective prompts can help streamline blockchain processes and provide insights into data stored in distributed ledgers.

Example prompts

1. **For supply chain tracking:** Analyse blockchain records to identify inefficiencies in the supply chain for a pharmaceutical product.
2. **For smart contracts:** Draft a smart contract for a freelance agreement with terms for milestone-based payments and automated escrow release.
3. **For decentralized finance (DeFi):** Summarize the potential risks of a new DeFi lending platform based on its blockchain transaction history.

Advanced prompt

Simulate a supply chain audit using blockchain data for a logistics company. Include analysis of tamper-proof records to recommend fraud prevention measures.

---

[7]**Note:** Use with caution. AI can provide guidance but is no replacement yet for actual skill and knowledge.

3. AR/VR: Interactive prompts for immersive experiences

AR and VR are revolutionizing industries from gaming to education. Prompts can design immersive experiences tailored to user needs and preferences.

Example prompts

1. **For retail experiences:** Create an AR experience for an Indian fashion retailer that allows customers to virtually try on sarees.
2. **For training simulations:** Develop a VR training module so that first responders can conduct disaster management mock drills.
3. **For education:** Design an AR application to teach children about Indian wildlife through interactive 3D visuals.

Advanced prompt

Generate a VR learning environment for architecture students that visualizes historical Indian monuments, incorporating real-world dimensions and textures for immersive exploration.

4. Autonomous systems: Efficient prompts for smart operations

Autonomous systems like drones, self-driving cars and robotics rely on precision and adaptability. Prompts can optimize their operation by analysing real-time data and improving decision-making.

Example prompts

1. **For drone deliveries:** Plan the most efficient drone delivery route for packages in a densely populated urban area, considering weather and traffic conditions.
2. **For self-driving cars:** Simulate a traffic flow optimization

model using data from autonomous vehicles in Mumbai during peak hours.

3. **For robotics in manufacturing:** Optimize the workflow of robotic arms on an assembly line to reduce production time and material waste.

Advanced prompt

Develop a predictive maintenance schedule for a fleet of autonomous delivery drones using real-time telemetry data to minimize downtime and operational costs.

5. Integrating emerging technologies with AI prompts

As these technologies converge, integrating them with AI amplifies their potential. Effective prompts can connect data streams from IoT devices, blockchain systems, AR/VR environments and autonomous systems for unified solutions.

Example prompts

1. **Cross-technology integration:** Combine IoT and blockchain data to create a real-time dashboard tracking inventory and validating its authenticity.
2. **Smart city planning:** Develop an integrated AR application using IoT sensors to visualize real-time traffic and air quality in Jaipur for urban planning.
3. **Healthcare innovations:** Design a solution that uses IoT devices and VR simulations to monitor and rehabilitate patients with mobility challenges.

Advanced prompt

Propose a holistic solution that integrates IoT, blockchain, and VR for disaster response, enabling real-time data sharing, transparent supply chain tracking and immersive training simulations for emergency teams.

6. Why mastering prompts for emerging technologies matters

The ability to interact with emerging technologies through well-crafted prompts:

- **Drives innovation:** Enables creative problem-solving and optimized workflows.
- **Improves accessibility:** Makes advanced technologies usable for individuals and businesses without technical expertise.
- **Fosters collaboration:** Bridges gaps between different technologies for holistic solutions.
- **Enhances impact:** Amplifies the potential of these technologies to address global challenges, such as sustainability and inclusivity.

Mastering prompts for emerging technologies is not just a technical skill but a strategic advantage in today's world. By learning to harness IoT, blockchain, AR/VR and autonomous systems, individuals and organizations can unlock new possibilities, drive innovation and create meaningful impact.

19

Mastering Multilingual Prompts

The diversity of languages across the world, particularly in multilingual nations like India, presents both challenges and opportunities in effective AI communication.

Multilingual prompt engineering is about crafting inputs that cater to multiple languages while maintaining accuracy, cultural relevance and inclusivity. This chapter explores techniques, strategies and advanced prompts to unlock the potential of AI for multilingual applications.

ChatGPT, Gemini, Copilot and other similar tools can do this task very well.

1. Translation and localization

Scenario: You need to ensure high-quality translations that are culturally relevant and contextually accurate.

Prompt

Assume you are an AI translation expert specializing in Indian languages. Translate the following English paragraph into Hindi, ensuring that all idiomatic expressions are localized appropriately. Additionally, adapt the tone to be formal and respectful for a government audience.

Scenario: Create multilingual content for a website that engages a culturally diverse audience.

Prompt

Generate content for an e-commerce website homepage. The content should highlight a Diwali sale in English, Hindi and Tamil. Maintain a festive tone, ensure cultural appropriateness for each language and optimize for SEO keywords relevant to each regional market.

2. Multilingual customer support

Scenario: A customer service chatbot needs to handle queries in multiple languages.

Prompt

Design a multilingual customer support chatbot script for an Indian telecom company. The chatbot should detect the user's language (English, Hindi, Kannada) from the first message and respond accordingly. Include pre-written replies for billing queries, technical issues and new connections.

Scenario: Ensure accuracy and empathy in multilingual responses for sensitive topics.

Prompt

Create empathetic responses for a customer service chatbot addressing late payment issues. Write these responses in English, Hindi and Bengali, ensuring the tone remains understanding and supportive in all languages.

3. Language-specific challenges

Scenario: Tackle grammatical and structural differences across languages.

As a linguistic expert, rewrite the following product description in Marathi, Gujarati and English. Ensure each version adheres to the grammatical rules and natural flow of the target language while retaining the core message and tone.

Scenario: Address the complexities of formal versus informal communication in languages.

Prompt

Create two versions of an appointment confirmation email for a hospital. One version should be in formal Tamil for older patients, and the other in informal Punjabi for younger patients. Ensure the tone matches the audience demographics while maintaining clarity.

4. Multilingual AI training

(**Note:** This is for engineers who would like to design their own SLM or LLMs.[8])

Scenario: Fine-tune an AI model for multilingual text classification.

Prompt

Design a training dataset for an AI model that classifies customer reviews in English, Hindi and Telugu. Specify the types of data samples, class labels and the balance required across languages to ensure accurate classification results.

Scenario: Improve an AI model's ability to generate culturally relevant multilingual content.

---

[8]Small language models (SLMs) have fewer parameters and are fine-tuned on a subset of data for a specific use case. Large language models (LLMs) are trained on large-scale datasets and usually require large-scale cloud resources.

Develop a fine-tuning strategy for an AI model that generates festival greetings in multiple Indian languages. The model should adapt its tone and content to the cultural nuances of each language (e.g., use Tamil-specific traditions for Pongal and Gujarati-specific customs for Navratri).

5. Cross-language collaboration

Scenario: Enable collaborative projects across language barriers.

Prompt

Create a multilingual meeting summary template. Assume a business meeting was conducted with participants speaking English, Hindi and Bengali. Generate a summary in each language, ensuring that key decisions and action items are clear and consistent across all versions.

Scenario: Facilitate multilingual project documentation for teams.

Prompt

Draft a project update document for a software development team. The document should include key milestones in English, progress reports in Kannada and risk assessments in Hindi. Ensure all sections are consistent in tone and format.

6. Enhancing inclusivity with multilingual prompts

Scenario: Make AI more inclusive by addressing accessibility in multiple languages.

Prompt

Design audio prompts for visually impaired users in English, Hindi and Malayalam. The audio content should guide them through an online banking application with clear instructions, using a tone that is calm and reassuring.

Scenario: Bridge language gaps in rural and urban settings.

Prompt

Develop an educational chatbot script for farmers in rural India. The chatbot should answer agricultural queries in Hindi, Tamil and Marathi, ensuring the language is simple, contextually relevant and respectful of regional terminologies.

Why multilingual prompts matter

Mastering multilingual prompts is not just about translation— it's about inclusivity, precision and cultural understanding. These advanced prompts empower professionals to:

- Enhance customer engagement across languages.
- Develop culturally aware content that resonates with diverse audiences.
- Train AI systems for global and regional relevance.
- Break down language barriers in collaborative and operational settings.

By embracing multilingual prompt engineering, readers can make AI a tool that bridges divides and brings people closer together, regardless of the language they speak.

20

Exploring Future Roles for AI Prompts

As AI continues to evolve, the applications and potential of prompt engineering expand beyond the roles we see today. Emerging technologies and societal needs are creating entirely new possibilities where well-crafted prompts will play a pivotal role.

This chapter explores futuristic roles where prompt engineering could redefine workflows, decision-making and innovation. By understanding these roles, readers can prepare to lead in areas yet to be fully realized.

1. AI Coach for Personal and Professional Growth

An AI coach uses tailored prompts to guide individuals in personal development, career planning and skill enhancement. These coaches adapt to the user's needs, offering personalized strategies, motivational support and actionable insights.

Example prompts

1. Design a 30-day career development plan for a mid-level manager transitioning into a leadership role.
2. Generate a personalized exercise routine for a 40-year-old professional with limited time.
3. Create a study schedule for a student preparing for competitive exams, balancing intensive study sessions with adequate breaks.

Future potential

AI coaches could integrate with wearable devices to track real-time health and productivity metrics, refining prompts to optimize well-being and efficiency.

Advanced prompt

Design a career coaching programme that adapts dynamically to the user's performance data, integrating feedback from assessments and real-time inputs like productivity and stress levels. Ensure the recommendations align with the user's long-term career goals and daily habits.

2. Conversational Designer for Virtual Personas

A conversational designer creates virtual personas or chatbots that interact naturally and contextually with users. These personas could represent brands, educators or even fictional characters.

Example prompts

1. Develop a conversational script for a virtual assistant helping users file taxes in India.
2. Design dialogue for a museum guide chatbot that engages visitors with interactive storytelling about Indian history.
3. Create a personality and conversational flow for a chatbot offering mental health support.

Future potential

Incorporating AI into immersive AR/VR environments, conversational designers could build avatars that interact with users in real-time, enhancing customer experiences and education.

Advanced prompt

Design a virtual persona for an e-commerce platform that adapts its tone and recommendations based on user demographics, preferences and purchase history. Ensure the persona feels consistent and engaging across voice, text and visual interactions.

3. AI Governance and Ethics Consultant

An AI governance consultant focuses on crafting prompts that ensure AI systems operate ethically and inclusively, adhering to global standards and local regulations.

Example prompts

1. Generate guidelines for a financial AI system to detect biases in loan approval algorithms.
2. Create an AI model audit checklist for an educational platform ensuring fairness in student assessments.
3. Draft a code of ethics for an AI system interacting with children in learning applications.

Future potential

As AI becomes integral to governance, consultants will work on integrating ethical safeguards directly into system prompts to minimize misuse and bias.

Advanced prompt

Develop a compliance framework for AI systems operating in multilingual regions, ensuring that all outputs are free from cultural, linguistic and social biases. Include dynamic checks for evolving ethical concerns.

4. Prompt Architect for Dynamic Workflows

A prompt architect designs multi-step prompts to automate complex workflows, combining AI capabilities across multiple domains.

Example prompts

1. Create a multi-step workflow for generating market analysis, including data collection, trend analysis and reporting.
2. Design a prompt chain for a hospital management system to coordinate patient records, appointment scheduling and billing.
3. Develop an automated process for legal document drafting and review with AI guidance.

Future potential

Prompt architects will play a key role in building integrated systems for smart cities, healthcare and supply chain optimization, enhancing cross-functional collaboration.

Advanced prompt

Design an end-to-end workflow for a smart city's AI system that integrates data from IoT devices, traffic monitoring and citizen feedback to optimize urban planning decisions. Ensure prompts adjust dynamically based on real-time inputs.

5. AI Content Curator for Personalized Media

An AI content curator uses prompts to create and recommend highly personalized media experiences, including articles, videos and podcasts.

Example prompts

1. Generate a personalized news feed for a tech enthusiast focusing on AI and blockchain.
2. Curate a playlist of podcasts about entrepreneurship tailored for early-stage start-up founders.
3. Create a recommendation list of books and movies for someone interested in historical fiction.

Future potential

Content curators could leverage AI to design entire personalized media ecosystems, blending user preferences, mood analysis and emerging trends.

Advanced prompt

Develop a personalized learning path for a student interested in AI ethics, combining articles, video lectures and hands-on tutorials. Tailor the recommendations based on their prior knowledge and learning pace.

Why future roles matter

These emerging roles illustrate the vast potential of prompt engineering in redefining how we interact with technology. From enhancing productivity to fostering inclusivity, mastering these future-oriented applications of prompts will ensure individuals remain at the forefront of innovation. As these roles evolve, the principles of adaptability, creativity and ethical responsibility will remain central to their success.

21

Creating the Most Advanced Prompts

To master prompt engineering, one must evolve beyond simple inputs to craft highly advanced prompts that integrate role-specific expertise, context, ethical considerations and dynamic adaptability.

Advanced prompts are designed to optimize AI responses, handle complex tasks and create seamless human–AI interactions. This chapter delves into crafting the most advanced prompts by combining multiple dimensions, such as role clarity, scope, boundaries, specifics, tone and multi-step processes.

Framework for crafting advanced prompts

1. **Role definition:** Clearly specify the AI's role (e.g., analyst, assistant, teacher) to align its response style.
2. **Scope and boundaries:** Define the task's scope while setting clear boundaries to avoid irrelevant or biased outputs.
3. **Specifics:** Include granular details like data inputs, desired output format and any rules the AI must follow.
4. **Context integration:** Provide background or situational context to ensure AI tailors its response appropriately.
5. **Ethics and tone:** Specify ethical guidelines and the tone for the response to match the target audience.

Multidimensional business strategy

Scenario: A company wants to launch a new product in a highly competitive market. The goal is to create a comprehensive business strategy that integrates market research, consumer behaviour analysis, pricing models and marketing plans.

Prompt

Assume you are a business strategist working for a start-up entering the wearable health technology market in India. Your task is to design a comprehensive product launch strategy. Use the following considerations to structure your response.

1. **Role:** Act as a business strategist with expertise in technology-driven healthcare markets.
2. **Scope:** Focus on India, targeting urban and semi-urban populations. Include competitive analysis, pricing models and marketing strategies.
3. **Boundaries:** Avoid relying solely on generic market data; ensure recommendations are tailored to the Indian market, considering cultural nuances and affordability.
4. **Specifics:**
   » Market research: Analyse potential competitors, target demographics and regional trends.
   » Consumer behaviour: Highlight factors like digital literacy, health awareness and buying power.
   » Pricing strategy: Suggest pricing tiers to accommodate varied income groups.
   » Marketing plan: Propose channels and messaging for urban (social media, influencers) and semi-urban areas (local campaigns, healthcare partnerships).
5. **Ethics and tone:** Ensure inclusivity in messaging, avoiding any bias related to socio-economic status or regional disparities. Maintain a professional and approachable tone.

Expected output

1. **Market overview:**
   » Competitors: Identify key players (e.g., international brands and local start-ups).
   » Trends: Highlight growing demand for affordable health tech due to post-pandemic health awareness.
2. **Target demographics:**
   » Urban consumers: Tech-savvy professionals aged 25–40.
   » Semi-urban consumers: Health-conscious families with moderate digital exposure.
3. **Pricing model:**
   » Basic model: Affordable features, targeting semi-urban buyers (~₹3,000–₹5,000).
   » Advanced model: Premium features for urban professionals (~₹10,000+).
4. **Marketing plan:**
   » Urban: Partner with fitness influencers and run digital campaigns on Instagram and YouTube.
   » Semi-urban: Collaborate with local health clinics and use WhatsApp for community-driven campaigns.
5. **Ethical considerations:**
   » Avoid pricing that excludes lower-income groups.
   » Ensure that marketing emphasizes health benefits without unrealistic claims.

Multi-step advanced prompt for smart cities

Scenario: Design an AI-powered smart city solution to improve urban mobility, reduce energy consumption and enhance citizen well-being.

As a smart city consultant, design an AI-driven solution to optimize urban mobility and energy consumption for a metropolitan area. Address the following key dimensions:

1. **Role:** Assume the role of a smart city strategist integrating AI, IoT and data analytics.
2. **Scope:** Focus on urban mobility, energy efficiency and citizen engagement.
3. **Boundaries:** Ensure solutions align with environmental sustainability goals and are affordable for public infrastructure budgets.
4. **Specifics:**
   » Urban mobility: Develop traffic management systems using real-time data.
   » Energy consumption: Optimize energy grids with predictive analytics.
   » Citizen engagement: Suggest AI-driven platforms for collecting public feedback and improving city services.
5. **Ethics and tone:** Ensure transparency in data usage and inclusivity in citizen engagement. Maintain a visionary yet practical tone.

Expected output

1. **Urban mobility solution:**
   » AI-powered traffic lights adapting to congestion patterns.
   » Real-time public transport updates via a mobile app.
2. **Energy efficiency plan:**
   » Predictive analytics for optimizing electricity distribution based on usage patterns.
   » Solar energy integration for public buildings to reduce grid dependency.

3. **Citizen engagement platform:**
   » An app for reporting issues (e.g., potholes, waste collection) with real-time tracking.
   » Gamified features encouraging citizens to contribute ideas for city improvement.
4. **Ethical safeguards:**
   » Data privacy policies that ensure citizen data security.
   » Inclusive design for accessibility in multiple languages.

Why advanced prompts matter

Advanced prompts bridge the gap between generic AI responses and highly specialized solutions. By incorporating multi-dimensional details, they

- deliver precise, actionable outputs tailored to complex tasks.
- reflect real-world expertise, enhancing the utility of AI.
- ensure ethical and inclusive AI applications across domains.

22

Expanding the Boundaries of Prompt Engineering

In this chapter we will talk about the forward-thinking and exploratory nature of the ideas presented, emphasizing how the book invites readers to imagine the untapped potential of AI and its transformative impact across industries and individual lives.

1. AI in human creativity: Unleashing artistic potential

- **Why:** To highlight the lesser-discussed intersection of AI and human creativity.
- **What to include:**
  - » Prompts for creating art, music, poetry, storytelling.
  - » Case studies where AI has been used to co-create with artists.
  - » Ethical considerations of AI-generated creative works.

Advanced prompt

As a collaborative artist, use AI to co-create a painting description based on the theme of 'Unity in Diversity', tailored for an art exhibition in India. Ensure the tone reflects cultural harmony.[9]

2. The future of work: AI-augmented team collaboration

- **Why:** To explore how AI can redefine teamwork and collaboration.

---

[9]You can try this prompt on ChatGPT or Copilot.

- **What to include:**
  - » Prompts for team dynamics, virtual collaboration and remote work challenges.
  - » AI-driven role assignments and workload balancing.
  - » Future scenarios of AI-coordinated team efforts.

Advanced prompt

Design a team collaboration workflow where AI assigns tasks based on individual strengths and availability for a multinational project launch. Include metrics for balancing workload and ensuring fair task distribution.

3. Cultural sensitivity in AI prompts

- **Why:** To emphasize inclusivity and avoid cultural biases in AI-generated outputs.
- **What to include:**
  - » Prompts that adapt to regional, linguistic and cultural nuances.
  - » How to detect and mitigate cultural insensitivity in AI outputs.
  - » Practical examples for global businesses, diplomacy and education.

Advanced prompt

Create an onboarding guide for employees in a global company with offices in India, Japan and Germany. Ensure the guide respects cultural norms and communication styles unique to each region.

4. Personal productivity with AI prompts

- **Why:** To make AI relatable to individual users, enhancing their daily lives.

- **What to include:**
  - » Prompts for personal goal-setting, time management and habit tracking.
  - » Using AI for journaling, mindfulness and stress management.
  - » AI as a personal assistant for streamlining daily tasks.

Advanced prompt

Develop a personalized daily planner for a freelancer juggling multiple projects. The planner should prioritize tasks, include breaks and offer motivational tips.

5. Prompts for social good and sustainable development

- **Why:** To align the prompts with broader global goals like sustainability and social impact.
- **What to include:**
  - » Prompts for climate modelling, disaster response and resource optimization.
  - » AI in education for underprivileged communities.
  - » Tools for NGOs and policymakers using AI effectively.

Advanced prompt

Design an AI-driven community project to monitor and reduce plastic waste in coastal areas. Include prompts for data collection, volunteer coordination and public awareness campaigns.

6. Prompt failures: What goes wrong and how to fix it

- **Why:** To address a critical yet underexplored topic that resonates with users.
- **What to include:**
  - » Examples of common prompt failures and their root causes.

» Techniques to debug and refine ineffective prompts.

» Case studies of overcoming complex prompt challenges.

Advanced prompt

Explore a failed prompt scenario where AI-generated outputs consistently miss ethical guidelines for medical advice. Break down the issue and craft a refined prompt.

7. Gamification of prompt engineering

- **Why:** Gamification enhances learning by making the process engaging, interactive and rewarding. It encourages users to experiment with prompts, receive feedback and refine their skills in a fun way.
- **What to include:**
  » Quizzes and scenarios for readers to craft the best prompts.
  » Reward systems for learning milestones.
  » Role-based simulations (e.g., be a doctor, teacher, CEO).

Gamification example: Quiz

You are a customer service manager and need to write a prompt to get AI to draft a polite email for a refund request. Which is the best approach?

a) Write an email.
b) Create a short email requesting a refund politely, mentioning the order number and reason for return.
c) I need an email, make it now.

Advanced prompt

Assume the role of a city planner tasked with creating an AI-assisted urban design. Your goal is to maximize green spaces while accommodating a growing population. Submit your prompt for evaluation.

8. The ethics and philosophy of prompts

- **Why:** To add intellectual depth and provoke thought about the implications of AI usage.
- **What to include:**
  » Philosophical debates about human versus AI decision-making.
  » Ethical dilemmas in AI-assisted scenarios.
  » Guidelines for aligning AI use with human values.

Advanced prompt

Analyse the ethical implications of using AI to monitor employee productivity in real time. Suggest safeguards to ensure fairness and privacy.

9. Future-proofing prompts for evolving AI models

- **Why:** To prepare users for ongoing advancements in AI capabilities.
- **What to include:**
  » How prompts might evolve with more advanced AI models.
  » Techniques for crafting adaptable and scalable prompts.
  » Predictions for the role of natural language in future AI interactions.

Advanced prompt

Draft a future-proof AI prompt for content generation, ensuring it adapts seamlessly to new language models with improved contextual understanding.

23

Real-World Case Study

Scenario: Advanced AI-powered résumé hygiene check

◆

Context

You run a tech company and receive hundreds of résumés for various roles. To streamline the initial screening process and ensure high-quality candidates, you want to use AI to perform a hygiene check on résumés. This involves identifying anomalies, validating information against online profiles, extracting hobbies and interests, and conducting a basic internet search to flag any legal or political issues.

Assumptions

Note: These details are for illustrative purposes only.

1. **Résumé details**
   Candidate name: Arjun Sharma
   LinkedIn: https://linkedin.com/in/examplearjunsharma
   GitHub: https://github.com/examplearjun-code
   Facebook: https://facebook.com/examplearjunsharma
   Instagram: https://instagram.com/examplearjunsharma
   Most recent employers: VideoMeet Pvt Ltd, Data Xgen Technologies

2. AI's role

- Extract and cross-verify details from the résumé and online profiles.
- Identify mismatched or missing information between the résumé and LinkedIn.
- Extract hobbies and interests from all available profiles.
- Perform an internet search to flag any legal, political or controversial mentions.

Advanced prompt

You are an AI assistant tasked with performing a comprehensive hygiene check on résumés for a tech company. Your goal is to ensure the credibility of candidates by analysing their résumés and associated online profiles. Follow these steps for the candidate Arjun Sharma:

1. Extract key details from résumé: Parse and summarize the key information provided in the résumé (e.g., education, experience, skills, contact details).
2. Cross-verify details with LinkedIn: Access the LinkedIn profile provided in the résumé. Compare the job titles, company names, dates of employment and skills listed. Highlight any discrepancies.
3. Identify anomalies: Flag any unusual or inconsistent information, such as unexplained gaps in employment history or exaggerated credentials.
4. Extract hobbies and interests: Use Facebook, Instagram, and other social profiles to identify hobbies and interests that the candidate shares publicly. Summarize these in bullet points.
5. Conduct a comprehensive internet search: Perform a search using the candidate's name and the names of their most recent two employers (TechWave Solutions and DataMatrix, Inc.). Look for any mentions in news

articles, blogs, forums or legal databases. Highlight any references to legal cases, political affiliations or controversial activities.

6. Provide a final report: Summarize your findings in a structured format with these sections:
    » Key information from résumé
    » LinkedIn discrepancies
    » Anomalies in résumé
    » Hobbies and interests
    » Legal or political mentions
    » Overall recommendation

Ensure the tone is objective and professional.

Example output

Key information from résumé:
Name: Arjun Sharma
Most recent employers: VideoMeet Pvt Ltd (2019–2022), Data Xgen Technologies (2016–2019)
Skills: Python, machine learning, cloud computing, video conferencing, enterprise email
Contact details: arjun.sharma@exampleemail.com
LinkedIn discrepancies:

- Résumé lists 'Lead Developer' at VideoMeet, but LinkedIn shows 'Senior Developer'.
- Dates of employment for Data Xgen Technologies differ by three months between LinkedIn and the résumé.

Anomalies in résumé:

- Missing explanation for a six-month gap between college graduation and first job.
- Claims of contributing to a high-profile project not mentioned on GitHub or LinkedIn.

Hobbies and interests:

- Facebook: Photography, cricket
- Instagram: Travel blogger with a focus on Himalayan treks
- GitHub: Active contributor to open-source projects related to AI

Legal or political mentions:

- Internet search flagged a political blog post where the candidate criticized a controversial corporate policy while at a previous company.
- No legal cases or political affiliations found.

Overall recommendation: The candidate's profile has minor discrepancies but demonstrates strong technical skills and creativity. Further clarification on employment gaps and project claims is recommended during the interview process.

Why this prompt works

- Multidimensional approach: Covers all aspects of résumé hygiene, including validation, anomaly detection and public persona analysis.
- Granularity: Ensures specific instructions for each step to provide actionable insights.
- Customizable: Can be adapted for different industries, roles or company requirements.

Understanding LLMs and choosing the right one

As AI becomes a bigger part of our daily lives, many people assume all AI models function the same way. But the reality is quite different. Not all LLMs have live internet access, not all can generate images and their ability to process information varies significantly. Some excel in coding and reasoning, while others are designed for general conversations or business applications.

When I first started exploring LLMs, I realized how overwhelming it can be to choose the right one. Each model comes with its own strengths and limitations, and using the wrong one for a specific task can lead to frustration. So, let's break it down in a way that makes sense.

One of the most well-known and widely used AI models today is ChatGPT-4o by OpenAI. It is a highly capable, multimodal model that handles complex tasks such as reasoning, coding, language translation and dynamic conversation. GPT-4o now natively supports image generation, allowing users to create photorealistic visuals, illustrations, diagrams and even infographics directly within the chat using conversational prompts. It also excels at maintaining style and layout consistency across iterations and can handle text-in-image rendering with notable accuracy.

While GPT-4o doesn't have real-time internet access by default, it can fetch live data when connected to enabled browsing tools or external APIs. However, responses may not always reflect the latest events unless browsing is explicitly turned on.

If you need a model that can search the web in real time, then Google's Gemini is a better choice. Unlike ChatGPT, Gemini has live internet access and is also multimodal, meaning it can process not just text but also images and, in some cases, audio. This makes it an excellent option for research and real-world applications where up-to-date information is crucial.

For those who want AI that can handle long, detailed reasoning, Claude 3.7 Sonnet by Anthropic is a strong contender. Claude is built with a focus on safety, accuracy and deep contextual understanding. It's particularly useful for businesses, coding, long-form content creation and cases where accuracy is more important than creativity.

If your priority is coding and AI development, then Mistral 7B, Mixtral or Llama 3 are great open-source options. These models are designed with developers and businesses in mind, offering fast performance without the constraints of proprietary models like ChatGPT or Gemini. Open-source AI is especially useful for companies that want more control over their AI applications.

For people looking for factually accurate answers and deep retrieval capabilities, Command R+ by Cohere is another interesting model. It is built with retrieval-augmented generation, meaning it can fetch and summarize information more effectively than other models that rely solely on their internal knowledge.

How to choose the right model

When people ask me which AI model they should use, I always tell them: it depends on what you need.

- If you need real-time internet access, go with Gemini.
- If you want balanced performance with strong reasoning and image generation, ChatGPT-4 Turbo is a great choice.
- If long-form content and deep analysis are your priorities, Claude 3.7 Sonnet is a solid option.
- If you prefer open-source AI, then Mistral, Mixtral or Llama 3 will serve you well.
- If you're working with AI for business intelligence and research, Command R+ is worth exploring.

Many people assume AI is a one-size-fits-all solution, but every LLM has a specific role. Understanding their differences allows you to get the most out of AI tools and avoid frustration. Whether you're using AI for business, creativity or problem-solving, choosing the right model is the first step in mastering prompt engineering.

Acknowledgements

I want to extend my heartfelt gratitude to those who contributed to shaping this book.

Krupa Sriniwas from Puerto Rico, Tracey from Durban and Schalk Kearney from Cape Town helped me refine and enhance the prompts.

My son, Rishab Data, played a crucial role in redrafting the context of prompts to ensure clarity and understanding.

Glossary

Artificial Intelligence (AI): The simulation of human intelligence processes by machines, especially computer systems, which include learning, reasoning and self-correction.

Chain-of-Thought Prompting: A technique that guides the AI to break down a complex problem into logical steps, helping it provide accurate and reasoned answers.

Comparison Prompts: Prompts that ask AI to evaluate two or more options or perspectives, often used for decision-making and analysis.

Constraint-based Prompts: Prompts that include specific limitations, such as word count or format, to guide AI in delivering a tailored response.

Context: Information included in a prompt to help AI understand the background or setting, leading to more accurate and relevant answers.

Embedding: A way of representing text, images or other data in vector format, which AI models use to understand the content's context and meaning.

Few-Shot Prompting: A method of providing AI with a few examples in a prompt to clarify the expected response's tone, format or style.

Generate Knowledge Prompting: A strategy that asks AI to generate background knowledge before answering a question, providing context for more accurate responses.

Machine Learning Model: A computational model trained on data to make predictions or generate responses, used widely in AI applications, including prompt engineering.

Meta Prompting: A prompt style where AI is asked to generate additional prompts or suggestions, useful for brainstorming and exploring various approaches to a topic.

Narrative or Creative Prompts: Prompts designed to encourage imaginative responses, commonly used in story writing, ideation and other creative tasks.

Natural Language Processing (NLP): A branch of AI focused on enabling computers to understand and generate human language, foundational in prompt engineering.

Prompt Chaining: Linking multiple prompts in sequence, where each prompt builds on the previous response, ideal for multi-step or complex tasks.

Prompt Engineering: The process of designing prompts or instructions to guide AI systems in producing relevant, accurate and contextually appropriate responses.

Reflexion: A method that encourages AI to review and refine its previous answers, which helps improve response quality and completeness.

Retrieval-Augmented Generation (RAG): An approach where external information is brought into AI's response, helping it provide more accurate or up-to-date answers.

Role-based Access Control (RBAC): A system used in software where user permissions are based on their role, mentioned here as an example in developing secure AI prompts.

Role-playing Prompts: A prompt style that assigns AI a specific 'role' (e.g., 'nutritionist', 'project manager'), helping it respond from a specialized perspective.

Self-Consistency: A technique of generating multiple AI responses to the same prompt to identify the most consistent or reliable answer, enhancing accuracy.

Structured Prompting: Breaking down complex instructions into clear, sequential steps to guide AI, ensuring responses meet multi-part requirements.

Token: A unit of language (e.g., word or character) that an AI model processes; understanding token limits can help in creating concise prompts.

Tone: The specific style or attitude conveyed in a response, which can be customized in prompts (e.g., formal, friendly) to match the intended audience.

Tree of Thoughts: A technique for exploring multiple possible solutions or perspectives on a topic, useful for brainstorming and problem-solving.

UX/UI Design: User experience (UX) and user interface (UI) design, crucial for creating intuitive, visually appealing software interfaces, often referenced in technology prompts.

Zero-Shot Prompting: A prompting technique where AI is given no prior examples or context, relying solely on its general knowledge to respond.

Made in the USA
Monee, IL
07 July 2026

56551331R00135